Career Launcher

Recording Industry

Career Launcher series

Advertising and Public Relations
Computers and Programming
Education
Energy
Fashion
Film
Finance
Food Services
Hospitality
Internet
Health Care Management
Health Care Providers
Law
Law Enforcement and Public Safety
Manufacturing
Nonprofit Organizations
Performing Arts
Professional Sports Organizations
Real Estate
Recording Industry
Television
Video Games

Career Launcher

Recording Industry

By Don Rauf

Checkmark Books
An imprint of Infobase Publishing

Career Launcher: **Recording Industry**

Copyright © 2010 by Infobase Publishing, Inc.

All rights reserved. No part of this book may be reproduced or utilized in any form or by any means, electronic or mechanical, including photocopying, recording, or by any information storage or retrieval systems, without permission in writing from the publisher. For information contact:

Checkmark Books
An imprint of Infobase Publishing
132 West 31st Street
New York NY 10001

Library of Congress Cataloging-in-Publication Data

Rauf, Don.
    Recording industry / by Don Rauf.
        p. cm. — (Career launcher)
    Includes bibliographical references and index.
    ISBN-13: 978-0-8160-7955-1 (hardcover : alk. paper)
    ISBN-10: 0-8160-7955-2 (hardcover : alk. paper)
    ISBN-13: 978-0-8160-7977-3 (pbk. : alk. paper)
    ISBN-10: 0-8160-7977-3 (pbk. : alk. paper) 1. Sound
recording industry—Vocational guidance. I. Title.
    ML3790.R39 2010
    781.49023—dc22

                                                          2009050611

Checkmark Books are available at special discounts when purchased in bulk quantities for businesses, associations, institutions, or sales promotions. Please call our Special Sales Department in New York at (212) 967-8800 or (800) 322-8755.

You can find Ferguson on the World Wide Web at http://www.fergpubco.com

Produced by Print Matters, Inc.
Text design by A Good Thing, Inc.
Cover design by Takeshi Takahashi
Cover printed by Art Print Company, Taylor, PA
Book printed and bound by Maple Press, York, PA
Dated printed: May 2010

Printed in the United States of America

10 9 8 7 6 5 4 3 2 1

This book is printed on acid-free paper.

Contents

Foreword

Recently I listened to the morning radio on my commute to Masterdisk, and I was knocked off my seat to hear that sound recording engineers were among the hot jobs. I was surprised to hear that because the music industry has become so decentralized. Once, there were only a couple of major recording studios in each city; now there are dozens of home studios in every town, and many of those home studios operate like a commercial studio, recording albums for artists.

Masterdisk began in 1973 as the recording, editing, and mastering arm of Mercury Records, and I began as an intern at Masterdisk in 1983. I was hired in 1984 as an assistant. I later became Masterdisk's chief engineer. I remained there until 1999, when I founded Scott Hull Mastering. Ten years later, I returned as the new owner of Masterdisk, combining my independent music mastering business with a series of song writing/production suites and a recording/mix room.

Masterdisk has engineered top-selling albums by Bruce Springsteen, Nirvana, Kid Rock, Steely Dan, Madonna, Whitney Houston, John Mayer, Smashing Pumpkins, The Rolling Stones, Jay-Z, Pearl Jam, The White Stripes, Santana, Phil Collins, Lenny Kravitz, the Beastie Boys, Elvis Costello, Aerosmith, AC/DC, Public Enemy, Prince, The Who, Talking Heads, and David Bowie, to name just a few!

The fact is the model for the music industry is changing. The major record labels are not as big as they once were, mostly because CD sales have dropped as digital music downloads have increased. Musicians who once sold 100,000 of every album now have to be happy selling 8,000–9,000 copies. The record industry has not quite figured out how to make money—or as much money—selling songs downloaded from the Internet instead of selling albums in stores. The viral networking capability of the Web has made it easy for people to copy and share songs and not pay for them. You have to ask yourself: What kind of business is there if no one is exchanging money for the product, and how much does the quality of the product suffer if people are not getting paid? The quality of music is going to suffer if artists are not paid for their songs, because there is no financial incentive to make a good music product. I have heard that today some hot singles sell well on the day they are released, but then sales quickly plummet because of illegal file sharing on the Internet.

On the plus side, file sharing has gotten people excited about music again. Everyone is carrying around a portable music device. Nearly everyone is using social networks to find cool new music and share it with their friends. Years ago we did the same with our LPs, but we could not share them with 10 million people simultaneously. We have not seen such widespread interaction with music since the introduction of the Walkman in 1979. This invention allowed people to make their music-listening experience portable. Freed from the confines of their homes, they could enjoy music wherever they went: on subways, airplanes, and walks in their neighborhoods. Then the novelty of the Walkman wore off. For a long stretch, people lost the personal, portable connection with music. Compact discs did not travel as well as cassettes and tended to skip when played in Discmans, the CD equivalent of the Walkman. Now the new technology of mp3s and iTunes has gotten people excited again about music. The Internet has made it easy for people to explore music online and download the music that interests them most. Digital devices such as iPods are very transportable and can store massive catalogs of music.

The recording industry has definitely had trouble adjusting to the new technology and the Internet Age. Industry leaders have had to think differently. Apple is a good example of a company that proved the adjustment was possible. With the introduction of iTunes in 2001, Apple said, "This is what will make people excited about music again. Give people a player that is totally cool and easy to use. Make songs that are available at an affordable price so that artists and record labels get paid a little money." Apple's iTunes has become a new working model for the changing music technology.

I think there are lots of job opportunities out there, but job seekers have to think differently, too. You may find work doing sound design on a computer game or audio engineering for a satellite radio station. I know a sound engineer who mixes the live audio feed for *Emeril Live!* on the Food Network. It is broadcast audio, and since it is a live feed, it is like mixing a concert—warts and all. He records several episodes of the show in one workday. It is a live band, live audience, and it is mostly unscripted. It is definitely a niche job in the recording industry, but if you think creatively, you can find unique positions out there.

Because of new technology, the recording industry needs people who are specifically trained in archiving digital media. There is a distinct need for individuals who specialize in organizing, archiving, and accessing large-scale digital storage. I hear over and over from people who have lost creative product because they did not have the backup or the backup they thought they had was not good. Plus, you have to have all your audio tracks documented well or you just cannot find them. It is time to wake up to the need for digital archivists across the industry.

People in the industry are also looking for new revenue streams. I was working on a Lou Reed project, and we made him MP3 files and higher quality AAC files. Reed put both versions of the recordings for sale on his Web site, and the real audiophiles paid a higher price for the higher quality downloads. You can buy the resolution that fits your lifestyle, and with a high-speed modem, you can download the songs with the best audio quality in 15 or 20 minutes, as opposed to typical MP3, which may only take a minute to download. While many people want cheap or free digital downloads that are lower in quality, there is definitely a market for quality. The recording industry just has to figure out how to make it available to the consumer. There is a new opportunity for this type of service in today's recording industry. Those with the right technical know-how and business smarts may be finding employment in this area.

The recording industry will have a lot of opportunities in the future. Each year there are new music applications for cell phones, and television shows feature unique soundtracks that spotlight new artists. The Internet continues to get wider and faster, and personalized music delivery services like Pandora [Internet radio] will grow and offer different services. Through it all, there will be new technologies that professionals will have to master.

What will it take to succeed? It still all comes down to knowing what sounds good.

—Scott Hull
Owner and CEO, Masterdisk, New York City

Acknowledgments

Thank you to all the talented music business pros who provided invaluable assistance in writing this volume, especially:

Scott Hull, president/owner, Masterdisk in New York City.

Chris Butler, songwriter and performer with The Waitresses, and ace record producer.

Al Houghton, owner of Dubway Studios in New York City.

Matt Bien and Paul Goldberg, owners of Pure Audio, commercial recording studio in Seattle, Washington.

And extra special thanks to: Monique Vescia, my wonderful bee-raising, book-writing wife.

Introduction

The recording industry is definitely an industry in flux. The big record labels have been singing the blues with music sales at almost half of what they were in 2000, according to the Record Industry Association of America. Soundscan reports that only 112 albums released in 2008 sold more than 250,000 units that year and fewer than 200 artists broke 10,000 units for the first time. What's going on? What has changed the business so much? The answer is downloadable music and shareable digital music files. The computer age has made it incredible easy for consumers to copy and share music—often without paying for it.

The industry is gradually adjusting to this and other technological changes. If you are a creative professional starting out in the business and eager to learn new things, opportunities are growing. Consumer demand for music is high. Sales from digital music downloads are rising. Many in the industry—performers as well as executives—say that today's technological innovations have put the music business back in the hands of the music fans. Compressed digital audio files are quick to download and simple to share. They are easy to store on personal players, so music lovers can enjoy the music they like wherever they go. Apple has grown to become the frontrunner in digital music sales with its iTunes and iPods. Tens of millions of listeners are tuning into new media such as Internet radio and satellite radio. Legions of music lovers are watching music videos streamed into their computers via YouTube and other online services. Selling cell phone ringtones of popular songs is a multibillion dollar business. Digital home recording studios are springing up across the nation. *American Idol* is a smash television show. The National Association of Music Merchants reports that sales of musical instruments have been on the rise over the past 10 years. All these facts point to the demand for music and recordings.

Keep Up

Those who are looking for opportunities in the recording industry or a related field need to keep up with the evolving business. There are many ways to be involved in today's recording industry: For example, you might find a position marketing ringtones, or choosing cutting-edge music for a television show soundtrack, or designing the audio for a computer game, or deejaying on Internet radio.

In some ways, the technological advances of the Internet and digital music have put business back in the hands of the musicians. Musicians, home studios, and do-it-yourselfers are finding more ways to succeed on their own. It is easy to promote, distribute, and sell music via the Internet. If you have the entrepreneurial spirit, this may be a good time to promote your own music to the world.

At the same time, some of the more traditional opportunities in the recording industry are still there. Popular performing artists are still being signed to labels. Recording studios are still cranking out professional-quality recordings. The live concert business is booming, along with the sale of merchandise: T-shirts, hats, and other paraphernalia. The popularity of live concerts continues to support careers of live audio engineers, promoters, musicians, lighting technicians, and graphic designers who create the art for supporting merchandise.

Learn the Terrain

This book is designed to help workers in the recording industry find their path. The industry is undergoing a major transformation, and this book alerts readers to new cutting-edge career opportunities and to job positions that will remain in demand. Much of the book focuses on jobs directly related to making actual recordings. The foundation of this field still rests on creating quality audio recordings, so the book will focus on careers in the recording studio and the process of making audio recordings. Readers will find out what the different jobs are in a studio, what it is like to work in a recording studio, the equipment involved, and terminology. The book also highlights career opportunities for those who make and play music. Without them, there would be no sounds to be recorded in the first place. Also reviewed are job opportunities indirectly related to the field—in accounting, law, graphic design, and other areas that support the creation, recording, marketing, and distribution of music.

Readers who are already working in this field can explore the many occupational possibilities and better define their own career path. For each career, they will learn about the skills needed to succeed, and the additional education that is required or helpful. Someone working now as a recording technician may advance by taking courses to gain proficiency in recording software such as Pro Tools, for example.

In today's job market, the path to success may not be a straight one. You need to explore, and sometimes you may have to make lateral moves. Occasionally, you might have to shift into a lower level position to get on the track to your ultimate career goal. This book will give you advice on when and how to take advantage of these lower-level positions. Taking a position as a recording technician can put you on course to becoming a full-fledged engineer. Working as an assistant to sound designer in a computer games firm can lead to an eventual career as a sound designer for games. Professionals looking to advance need to know best approaches to getting ahead. The book offers pointers on setting up a mentorship and how to get the most out of it. Mentorships allow you to form a professional relationship with someone who has years of experience in the recording industry and can share their knowledge and perhaps offer networking opportunities. Legendary producer Quincy Jones is said to have been the mentor to Michael Jackson. Producer Brian Eno has served as mentor to David Bowie and The Talking Heads. Readers also learn about the value of networking and how making a good impression early on through hard work, dedication, and enthusiasm can lift an individual higher in the ranks.

When you hear of an opportunity that sounds well matched to your talents and personality, you have to be ready to interview and you need a résumé that will impress an employer. If you really want a position but you do not have the exact skills needed, think of the transferable skills you have that may apply: experience with customer service, organization, computers, and other areas. Communication skills—both oral and written—are always highly prized. We direct young professionals in the recording industry to online resources where they may find job opportunities, and they learn to maximize the opportunities found in want ads, job clubs, and career fairs.

Networking

Like so many fields, networking is key in the recording industry. Mobility on the career ladder often depends on who you know. For recording engineers, building business often depends on bringing in clients to record, and this requires a great deal of social skills and networking. In this occupation, you are developing a reputation on a gig-to-gig basis, and professionals in the field who make hiring decisions will be evaluating you on the quality and performance you put into each project. To this end, knowing how to speak the language of the recording industry helps develop more professional respect from colleagues and superiors. As a glossary of terminology and definitions, including abbreviations and slang, the "Talk Like a Pro" section of this book should assist you in this process.

History

This volume also reviews the history of the recording industry. Having a sense of what came before gives perspective on the entire occupation. Plus, lessons can be learned by looking back on history. For example, developing technologies (especially affordable ones) tend to replace older technologies. The record player replaced the wax cylinder player in the early 1900s, and more recently, MP3 players have replaced portable cassette players. Since the early days of the music industry, young people have had a great influence in determining what's popular—from The Beatles, to grunge, to rap music. So those in the business try to stay attuned to what interests the youth market. While the recording industry has always been fiercely competitive, jockeying to sign artists who are the most popular or becoming popular, it has also been a field that fosters creativity. After all, creating good music and recordings is what this industry is all about.

After reading this book, you should have sense of

→ how the industry is changing
→ future and current career opportunities
→ skills needed for various positions
→ work environments and work etiquette
→ operations of a recording studio, as well as protocols followed and the jargon used in the business
→ techniques for advancing your career in the workplace
→ tips for getting your next position, including how to find work, handling the interview, dressing for success, and writing a strong résumé and cover letter
→ history of the industry
→ the most current state of the recording field, including latest technologies and trends
→ the wealth of resources available to advance in this career and find new opportunities

Although the music industry is not as robust as it was 10 years ago as it goes through this transitional stage, a comeback may be on the way. When radio was first introduced in the United States in the 1920s, record sales fell dramatically. Music lovers were hearing their music for free and not buying as much. Sound familiar? But, in time, radio became a vehicle to promote the music, and as Americans grew more affluent, they wanted to own the music to play on their home record players. Time will tell how the present transition in the recording industry finally settles, but it does appear that smaller companies and those with a do-it-yourself attitude may thrive as larger companies struggle to sustain the profitability of the past. "In the music business bigger is not necessarily better," says Chuck Kaye, the CEO of Dreamworks Music Publishing. "In fact, I believe smaller is actually better."

Chapter 1

Industry History

Although recording technology is associated with the entertainment industry (specifically the music industry), the earliest recording devices were scientific instruments devised to capture sound waves. In 1857, a French typesetter named Édouard-Léon Scott de Martinville invented a machine he called the *phonautograph*. Scott de Martinville wanted to study the pattern sound waves made on a sheet of paper blackened by the smoke of an oil lamp. His device used a cone-shaped horn to direct sound toward a flexible diaphragm positioned at its smaller end. The movements in the diaphragm, caused by sound waves, moved the point of a stylus (made from a pig's bristle), inscribing a line into a cylinder coated with "lampblack," a kind of powdery carbon deposit.

The Origins of Playback

The phonautograph was designed to record sound but not to play it back. The wavering lines inscribed by the stylus created a phonautogram, a visual representation of sound. One of Scott de Martinville's phonautograms, on a 9-by-24-inch sheet of rag paper, was found in nearly pristine condition in storage in France's patent office and the Académie des Sciences. In early 2008, scientists at the Lawrence Berkeley National Laboratory in Berkeley, California, were able to use the latest computer technologies to play back what Scott de Martinville had recorded on April 9, 1860: 10 seconds of a lone singer performing a bit of the French folk song "Au claire de la Lune." This aural artifact now represents the very first sound recording, predating Edison's achievements by 20 years.

In 1874, Alexander Graham Bell, best known as the inventor of the telephone, built a version of Scott de Martinville's phonautograph that used an actual human ear as a recording mechanism. Bell removed a piece of a cadaver's skull that included the inner ear and attached a stylus to its moving parts. Devices like these were only able to record small scraps of sound.

One of the first people to bring about the recording industry was Thomas Alva Edison, who recorded the first human voice on December 6, 1877. Edison used a cylinder covered in tin foil to capture the sound. The sound was etched into the tin and then could be played back by cranking the cylinder while a needle ran along the recorded track. The sound was amplified through a small megaphone speaker. Until Scott de Martinville's phonautogram was discovered, Edison's recording of himself reciting "Mary Had a Little Lamb" on such a cylinder was believed to be the first recorded sound.

On December 22, 1877, Edison walked into the offices of the journal *Scientific American* and demonstrated his "talking machine" to the staff; they were astonished when the invention inquired about their health, asked how they liked the phonograph, and bid them a good night. Of course, those questions were all prerecorded by Edison and played back on his talking machine. Edison first envisioned the device as a business machine to be used for stenography. In an 1878 list of uses for his new invention, musical entertainment was fourth on Edison's list, after stenography, phonographic books for the blind, and the teaching of elocution. In 1878 Edison secured the patent on his tinfoil phonograph.

Also in the 1880s, Charles Tainter invented the first lateral-cut record, which resembled modern-day vinyl records. While he had been able to make the records, Tainter had no practical way of playing them back. Tainter later teamed up with Chichester Bell to invent the "graphophone," which recorded by making a cut in a thin layer of bees' wax that was wrapped around a cardboard tube. Bell, Tainter, and Edison were soon competing in the commercial development of cylinder recordings when a third inventor entered the scene. Emile Berliner was perfecting the means to play music through flat circular discs, which were the forerunners of modern records. In 1887, Berliner demonstrated his gramophone, which played a flat circular record when hand-cranked. Originally made of glass, Berliner's disc was later fabricated of zinc and then hard rubber.

In 1888, Berliner began mass-producing rubber vulcanite discs of music for sale, while Edison was selling his cylinders, which played on a battery-powered phonograph. In 1889, Edward Easton, who had bought the rights from Bell and Tainter, launched the Columbia Phonograph Company, which sold treadle-powered graphophones (the Bell-Tainter device) and the cylinders that were played on them. (A treadle is a foot-operated pedal or lever for a circular drive.)

Early Commercial Efforts

The first "phonograph parlor" opened in San Francisco in 1889. Customers sat at a desk and spoke through a tube to order a selection of music for a nickel. The operator would play the customer's selection through another tube connected to a cylinder player in a room below. Around the same time, coin-operated music machines were being produced. In 1891, Albert Keller designed automatic phonographs with Edison technology; these were installed in arcades in many big cities and were an early form of the jukebox.

At the end of the 19th century, recording as an industry was truly being born as the general public was able to buy music that they could play in their homes. Edison's phonograph could be bought for $20; a smaller version called the Gem was priced at $7.50. One of the most popular cylinder recording artists during this period was John Philip Sousa and the United States Marine Band. In the early 1890s, Emile Berliner's U.S. Gramophone Company was taking off, selling 1,000 machines and 25,000 records. The first hard rubber discs were five inches in diameter and later went to seven inches.

In the early 1900s, cylinders and discs were fighting for the music-buyer's business. The earliest gramophone discs on the market cost about 60 cents each, while Edison sold his cylinders for 50 cents each, which helped him to claim a huge part of music sales. Thomas Lambert perfected a method to mass produce cylinder recordings, based on his 1900 patent to make "indestructible cylinders." While the courts upheld Lambert's patent, Edison drove Lambert's company (the Indestructible Phonograph Company) out of business through a series of expensive lawsuits that challenged Lambert as the originator of this technology.

For a while, it seemed as if the cylinder might be the form of recorded music that would predominate. The gramophone required much more power to run because it had a heavy tone arm and horn, which weighed down the device, while the cylinder had a lighter, floating reproducer, and so required less power to run. Berliner corrected the problems of the gramophone, however, and the many advantages of the discs caught on with the public, making the gramophone the industry leader. Unlike cylinders, discs could be easily stored on a shelf, plus they could have music on two sides. In addition, discs were more durable than cylinders, whose wax compounds were easily broken and wore out. Discs were also easier to manufacture than cylinders (cylinders were etched, while records were pressed), and records were easier to store since they were thin and flat. And though it may seem like a minor point, the disc had a black area in the center where information about the record could be printed so customers could easily identify and organize their music. For cylinders, on the other hand, record companies usually had a generic printed label on the outside of the package, with no indication of the identity of the individual recording inside. For a long time, the cylinders themselves had no visual identification. Eventually, information was impressed on an edge of the cylinder, but it was not as easy to read as a record label. The flat disc records played at around 78 revolutions per minute (rpm), and most discs made between about 1898 and the late 1950s played at that speed. By the early 1900s, records were the most popular form of recorded music and cylinders were dying out. Eventually, all music manufacturers, including Edison, produced only discs and disc players. This story repeats itself with every new technological revolution: throughout the history of recording, older technologies are continually displaced by newer ones. MP3 players took over the portable music business, replacing portable cassette players, such as the Walkman.

Fast Facts

Emile Berliner eventually sold his licensing rights to his gramophone patent and the method of making records to the Victor Talking Machine Company, which later became RCA. Victor had a very popular trademark logo of Nipper, a white fox terrier dog listening to a record player. The image came from a painting by Francis Barraud called "His Master's Voice." Nipper is a long-lasting logo. Even in the late 1990s, RCA was using a version of the logo—two "Nippers"—a grown dog and a puppy to advertise a new line of television models and camcorders.

The Modern Production System

By the turn of the twentieth century, the big three recording companies in the United States were Edison, Victor, and Columbia. Despite lawsuits over patents that embroiled the nascent industry, the big three were remarkably successful. Tim Brooks, an author who has written extensively on the history of the recording industry, estimates total U.S. cylinder and disc sales in 1900 at about 3 million copies. Enrico Caruso holds the distinction of becoming the first singer to record his voice on a gramophone disc. He made the recording in 1902 in a studio belonging to the Gramophone and Typewriter Company in New York. His recording of "Vesti la Gubbia" in 1907 became the world's first million-selling record and helped the gramophone record triumph over other competing technologies for recorded music.

The Invention of Radio

At the end of the 1800s, as the technology to manufacture and reproduce sound was being perfected, modern radio was also being born. Although it was not apparent at first, broadcast technology would become a vital part of the recording and music industry. In 1894 Guglielmo Marconi invented a spark transmitter with an antenna in Bologna, Italy. Although Marconi is often credited as the father of radio, one year prior, Nikola Tesla demonstrated the first complete radio transmitter and receiver system. However, Marconi proved better at establishing radio commercially than Tesla. In 1897, Marconi established the Wireless Telegraph and Signal Company and sold his invention for wireless telegraphy to shipping companies as a communication device. Tesla filed his own radio patent applications in the United States in 1897, and they were granted in 1900. The U.S. Patent Office rejected Marconi's first patent applications for radio in the early 1900s, citing Tesla. In 1901, Marconi demonstrated the first broadcast across the Atlantic (using Tesla's oscillator), and in 1904 the Patent Office reversed its previous decisions and granted Marconi a patent for the invention of radio. However, in 1943, the Supreme Court upheld Tesla's original patent, confirming Tesla as the true inventor of radio. In time, radio would become the most popular way to hear and promote new music and help generate enormous sales of recordings, but in the early 1900s, the first commercial radio stations were still 20 years away.

Bringing Music into Homes

The turn of the twentieth century brought rapid advances in recording. Manufacturers found that shellac was better than vulcanite for making discs and could withstand wear from a heavy stylus, also called a phonograph needle. The players themselves became cheaper to produce and more people could buy them for their homes. In Denmark, Valdemar Poulsen patented the first magnetic recorder in 1898. It was a precursor to how recordings would eventually be made using magnetic tape. But Poulsen's magetic recorders at this stage were unreliable and more expensive than the wax cylinder phonographs. By 1904 International Talking Machines in Germany had mastered the technology to produce double-sided discs. International Talking Machines' label was called Odeon, and in 1909 Odeon released the first official album: four-double sided discs in a special package featuring Tchaikovsky's *Nutcracker Suite*.

Recorded music was becoming a part of people's homes. In 1906, Victor introduced a phonograph called the Victrola, which came in an enclosed wooden cabinet. The Victrola was a hit with consumers because the player looked like a piece of furniture that belonged in the home. The next five years brought progress in sound quality through improvements made to the speakers and the introduction of a diamond stylus. Victor held the patent on lateral cut records, but smaller labels began to argue that this technology was in the public domain and that they should be able to use it too. In the early 1920s, Gennett Record Company won a case that opened up Victor's technology to all record labels, and as a result more recordings and music were created.

Up until 1920, the music-loving consumer purchased cylinders or records to enjoy recorded music in the home, but commercial radio would add a new dimension. In Pittsburgh, on November 2, 1920, KDKA made the first commercial broadcast in the nation. The Westinghouse Electric & Manufacturing Company led the way in radio, opening up stations around the country over the next few years. Of course, consumers needed devices to hear these radio stations, and RCA and other companies begin to sell "radio music boxes." The year 1922 is known for the "broadcasting boom" with the construction of more than 500 broadcast stations. Manufacturers had trouble keeping up with the demand for receivers. Between 1923 to 1930 60 percent of American families purchased radios. While there were a variety of live broadcasts (news, radio plays, variety shows, and more), radio

Best
Practice

Owning the Music

Composers and musical artists in the early 1900s realized that their music was being duplicated and sold, and they wanted more protection and profit for the use of their music. In 1914 Victor Herbert found the American Society of Composers, Authors, and Publishers (ASCAP) to protect the copyrighted musical compositions of its members, who at the time included Irving Berlin, Jerome Kern, and John Philip Sousa. The organization helped to ensure that artists were paid properly for their work whether it was sold as sheet music, performed, or made into a recording. In the 1920s, as radio stations were built, ASCAP made sure its artists were paid for the broadcasting of their music. (If you are involved in the business of making songs and having them performed or broadcast, make sure you are affiliated with one of the performing rights organizations that collect royalties on your behalf.) Today, ASCAP continues to collect fees for artists and publishers for the broadcast and performance of songs and other musical pieces. Two other major organizations also formed to help artists and publishers collect royalties: BMI (Broadcast Music, Inc.) and SESAC (Society of European Songwriters, Artists and Composers).

stations also played records. At first, the new technology of radio led to a decline in record sales because people could hear music free on the radio, and they become less interested in actually buying music for their homes. The sales of records declined by about one half in the early 1920s, and some independent record companies that had come along went bankrupt or merged with other companies. You can see a parallel today as digital downloads have led to a decline in CD sales, and the industry is adjusting to the new business model.

Still, even with a decline, consumer interest in buying, owning, and playing music at home remained relatively strong. In 1923 Bessie Smith's blues music on her first record "Down-Hearted Blues" was a hit, selling 750,000 copies on the Columbia label. Also in 1923, Fiddlin' John Carson's "Little Old Log Cabin in the Lane" became the first hit country record.

Through the 1920s the technology of microphones and speakers improved, making sound recordings cleaner and of higher quality. Naturally, consumers valued better sound. Bing Crosby began recording in 1926, and over his career the famous crooner became a top recording artist, who recorded around 1,600 songs and sold around 400 million records. He was considered the first blockbuster music star, and he retains the record for recording the biggest selling song in history, 1942's "White Christmas," which has sold more than 35 million copies since its release. Crosby was also the number-one motion picture star from 1944 to 1949 and the number one radio star from 1931 to 1957. Crosby's success across many facets of the recording industry paved the way for all the later major pop stars like Elvis Presley, Michael Jackson, and Madonna.

Film Creates More Opportunities

In the mid 1920s, the first electronically recorded discs were produced; this technology, developed by AT&T and Western Electric, enabled filmmakers to record sound in sync with their filmed scenes. In 1927 *The Jazz Singer* debuted, starring Al Jolson. It was the first commercial sound film with recorded dialogue. Gradually recording voices, sounds, and music for movies became more sophisticated. The advent of sound in film paved the way for many sound engineering careers for composers, technicians, and others. The motion picture industry invested heavily in recording equipment, and movies became an important part of promoting music. In 1937 Disney released the first soundtrack album—the music and songs from *Snow White and the Seven Dwarfs*. Throughout film history, movies have made songs hits. Shirley Temple introduced the song "Good Ship Lollipop" in the 1934 movie *Bright Eyes*, and Mae Questal's cover of the song in the 1930s sold more than 2 million copies. Bing Crosby's "White Christmas" was introduced in the 1942 movie *Holiday Inn*. Many of the Bee Gees' biggest hits were part of the 1977 movie *Saturday Night Fever*. Most recently in 2009, the soundtrack to the movie *Twilight* was the number one album in the United States. Many stage musicals were made into movies and their soundtracks became top-selling albums, including *The Sound of Music, West Side Story*, and *Oklahoma*. And of course many films had their own unique soundtracks that became hits—*The Godfather, Purple Rain*, and *Star Wars*, to name a few.

Another device to play and distribute recorded music was the jukebox, which allowed patrons at restaurants, bars, and other venues to drop in a few coins to hear the latest music. In 1933 Wurlitzer became one of the main sellers of jukeboxes to taverns and other venues. In 1934 General George Squier came up with another unique way of disseminating music through a service called Muzak. The service eventually grew to become the biggest source of prerecorded music for stores, supermarkets, and malls.

The Changing Recording Technology

The recording studios of today got their start with the introduction of magnetic tape in the mid-1930s. The technology was patented in Germany at the beginning of the decade, and it was the first step in the road toward making multitrack tapes. These tapes have parallel bands or strips onto which engineers can record separate instruments— guitar, bass, drums, vocals, and more. Les Paul is generally credited with making the first multitrack recording around 1947, although he did this with acetate discs, not a magnetic tape. A song he recorded that year in his garage called "Lover (When You're Near Me)" featured Paul playing eight different parts on electric guitar. He recorded himself onto an acetate disc, then played the track while recording another track on top of it. He thus built his song layer by layer.

This idea of recording different instruments of different tracks really is the foundation of modern recording, where instruments are recorded on separate tracks and then an engineer or producer "mixes" the tracks together to make the desired overall song or sound. Whereas bands were recorded live in the past, multiple tracks let the artist record different instrument on different tracks. If a guitarist messed up a few notes in a solo, he or she could go back and record over the mistakes. With multitrack recording, the art of modern recording engineering came into existence. Engineers could edit and mix tracks together to get the sound they wanted. The new technology led to more experimentation as well, such as using effects like reverb and echo.

The record industry fell into a slump as a result of the economic strains of the Great Depression. That slump lasted until World War II, when there was a surge of interest in recording music to entertain both the troops and the people working on the home front. In 1942, Glenn Miller received the first ever "Gold Record" award from the Recording Industry Association of America for selling 1 million records with his hit song "Chattanooga Choo-Choo." While radio owners paid a little royalty to those who owned copyrights on songs, nothing was paid to musicians. Bandleader Fred Waring led the movement to have the broadcast industry pay royalties to musicians. This fight continues to this day in the United States. Proposed legislation before Congress in 2009, called the Performance Rights Act, would grant royalties to the performers when a song is broadcast. Broadcasters generally oppose the measure, saying that it would add to their costs and threaten their profitability. As of April 2010, this issue has yet to be resolved.

After the war, technology continued to progress. Improvements had been made to magnetic recording systems, and the technology flourished in the late 1940s. In 1948 microgroove technology and advances in plastics lead to long-playing records with low surface noise. Microgrooves were very fine grooves and many could be packed on a vinyl disc. The standard for long-playing albums became 33 1/3 rotations per minute (rpms), which is obviously slower than 78 rpms, allowing for the longer-playing album. In 1949 RCA debuted the seven-inch 45 rpm record, which became the standard for releasing single songs, generally about three to four minutes long. The late 1940s into the early 1950s also brought electric instruments to the public. The electric guitar, in particular, would soon change the face of music.

Rock 'n' Roll and the Youth Revolution

One of the biggest record-buying audiences has always been teenagers. After World War II, the influence of young people in society really took off, affecting language, music, clothing, and more. In 1947 six major labels controlled the industry (Columbia, Victor, Decca, Capitol, MGM, and Mercury), but teenagers were moving away from the mainstream as smaller, independent labels began putting out new and exciting music. In 1947 the artist Roy Brown produced one of the earliest rock 'n' roll records, "Good Rocking Tonight," on the small Sun Records label. In 1951 the Chess label released what Sam Phillips called the first rock 'n' roll record, "Rocket 88," written by Ike Turner and sung by Jackie Brenston. Radio station KOWH in Omaha, Nebraska, introduced Top 40 radio in the late 1940s, and by the 1950s rock 'n' roll was starting to push big bands and crooners like Bing Crosby off of the airwaves. In March 1952 radio disc jockey Alan Freed of Cleveland was credited for coining the phrase "rock 'n' roll." In 1954 Elvis Presley released "That's All Right," and a new pop superstar was on the rise.

In 1957 the National Academy of Recording Arts & Science was formed. As a way to recognize those who were creating the best recorded music, the organization began the Grammy Awards in 1959. "Volare" by Domenico Modugno won song of the year. Generally, winning a Grammy means more sales. (The sales of Bob Dylan's *Time Out of Mind* jumped more than 400 percent the week after it won Album of the Year at the 1997 Grammys.)

Music to Go—Transistor Radios and Cassettes

The technological foundations of transistor radios, cassette tape players, and reel-to-reel recorders capable of capturing sounds on up to four tracks were all laid during the late 1940s. These technological advancements laid the groundwork for another big trend that shaped the recording industry: portability. While some record players made in the late 1940s were easy to haul around and plug into a wall, the real movement toward portability started with the transistor radio. Transistors replaced the bigger vacuum tubes used in earlier radios. Transistor radios hit the commercial market in the mid-1950s and they quickly became a hit. Young consumers especially wanted their own portable radios and stereos, which were being sold in the late 1950s.

At the same time the record industry thought there might be a market for reel-to-reel prerecorded music, but it never caught on the way that LPs (long-playing records) did, and the format was considered a flop. However, inventors in the 1950s were also perfecting portable recorders like the Nagra and the Reporter tape recorder. In 1962 the Phillips Company of the Netherlands released the first compact audiocassettes, and soon after companies began selling

Fast Facts

Record labels did not release cassette singles or "cassingles" until almost 20 years after introducing cassette albums. One of the earliest cassingles was the song "Vacation" by the Go-Gos, released in 1982.

recorders that could record and play back sounds. Originally, manufacturers thought people would mostly use blank tapes for dictation or that reporters would use them to record interviews. They had the exact same wrong notion as Thomas Edison did when he introduced his recording device. Consumers eventually adopted the cassette to record music for personal listening, and making cassette compilations of songs almost became an art form with users.

By 1965 there were 2.5 million pre-recorded cassettes on the market. Mercury Records is credited with producing the first music cassettes and by 1968—the year that the Beatles released their first audiocassette, *Sgt. Pepper's Lonely Hearts Club Band*—most major labels were releasing their most popular artists on cassette as well as LP. Noise and hiss on tapes was a problem for listeners, but in 1969, Dolby Noise Reduction was introduced for pre-recorded tapes and it helped eliminate the annoying hiss. By amplifying the higher frequencies of the recorded music and lowering the constant noise, cassette playback became smoother and similar to record-album quality.

The cassette's popularity soared with the introduction of the Sony Walkman in 1979. This device allowed people to listen to their favorite music wherever they went. Many in the press were critical of the Walkman because it only played cassettes. There was no record function. The company marketed it to the young and stressed its portability and high audio quality. In 1979 the Walkman had sold 15,000 units. In 10 years Sony sold 50 million Walkmen. Eventually, *Walkman* became synonymous with *portable tape player*.

Consumers had an endless craving for portability, and the "boom box"—large and powerful but still portable sound systems —which first came along in the mid-1970s, became a top seller in the 1980s. Boom boxes became associated with rap, hip-hop music, and street life, and were given the nickname "ghetto blaster." Users carried them on their shoulder and would set them on the sidewalk and have impromptu break-dance sessions. Many were designed to pump up the bass to maximum. Although at first they were used to play cassettes, they were later adapted as CDs became the medium of choice for music lovers. More means to listen to music meant more music sales. High fidelity, low-cost recordings, a variety of music players, and American consumers with significant disposable income added up to increased music sales. In 1960 album sales stood at about $600 million but doubled to $1.2 billion by 1970.

The Influence of Television

In looking at the history of the recording industry, it is important to consider the impact of television. With legions of fans interested in rock 'n' roll in the 1950s, the radio scene was booming. This was also the decade when FM radio was introduced, providing listeners a higher quality of sound. (AM [amplitude modulation] radio is one group of radio frequencies and FM [frequency modulation] radio is another group. AM radio has a more limited dynamic and sound range.) But the 1950s also saw the development of videotape, and in 1956 CBS broadcast the first network television show on videotape, *Douglas Edwards and the News*, for a West Coast delay. Prior to this television shows were broadcast live. Television, like movies, would soon make more jobs for audio profession- als who could record the audio and handle the overall sound design of shows. Bands were introduced to wide audiences starting in the 1950s through shows like Dick Clark's *Ameri- can Bandstand*. Later music shows followed like *Soul Train* (debut 1971), *Don Kirchner's Rock Concert* (debut 1972), and *The Midnight Special* (debut 1972). Popular songs from tele- vision often became popular on radio and translated into more record sales. The theme from the television show *Mission Impossible* spent 14 weeks on Billboard's "Hot 100" in 1968. Other memorable TV theme songs that became top selling singles include the themes to *Hawaii 5-0* (1968), *M*A*S*H* (1972), and *The Greatest Ameri- can Hero* (1981).

Fast Facts

In the mid-1960s, the 8-track cartridge also became a popular format for listen- ing to music, especially in cars. The 8-track was invented by William Lear, who founded the Lear- jet aviation company. The 8-track had problems from the start. To fit an album onto an 8-track, it had to be split into four programs; this meant that songs were often chopped into two parts, that song orders were reshuffled, that some- times songs were repeated, or that there were long stretches of silence between songs. While the 8-track tapes were a hit for a while, by the late 1970s the public was abandoning the format in favor of cassettes and records. One of the last commercial releases on 8-track was Fleetwood Mac's *Greatest Hits* in 1988.

In the early to mid-1980s, another shift to the recording industry model came through tele- vision, as MTV, the music television network, took off. This cable television station was totally dedicated to showing music videos. Suddenly, music stars needed to know how to make videos as well as music to compete in the business. MTV became a huge publicity engine, and the biggest record sales began to go to the artists who were popular on MTV. Artists like Duran Duran, Prince, Michael Jackson, and Madonna catapulted to the top of the sales charts largely because of their popularity on MTV. More recently, mainstream television networks have been using new music on their programming on shows such as *Gossip Girl* and *One Tree Hill*. At the same time children's television programming has also made the careers of many pop stars, such as Miley Cyrus and Jonas Brothers. One of the most popular shows of the new century has been all about creating music stars, and it harkens back to the old day of the 1950s television talent shows. Simon Cowell has created a hit show finding new pop stars with the program *American Idol* (debut 2002).

Origins of Compact Discs and Digital Music

While tapes were having their moment in the sun with the Walkman, the music industry was about to be revolutionized again. In the late 1970s, Sony and Philips together assembled a team of engineers who designed the standard for the digital audio disc, called a compact disc or CD. The first commercial CD rolled off the presses in 1980, a recording of Richard Strauss's *Eine Alpensinfonie*. As with many new technologies, CDs were too expensive for most consumers when first introduced. A player could cost more than $2,000 in 1982. Player costs quickly dropped in the next few years to $350, and down to about $150 (and even lower) by the end of the decade. In 1984 the CD Walkman was on the market, and consumers could listen to their CDs in a portable form. In 1985 Dire Straits became the first artist to sell 1 million CDs with its album *Brothers in Arms*. Like the wax cylinder faded from popularity, vinyl records and cassettes soon began to be replaced by CDs. In 1988 CDs outsold LPs for the first time, and LP sales continued to drop significantly as the CD format grew in popularity.

The major technological change between LPs and cassettes and CDs is that the music information on CDs is digital rather than analog. Analog is a type of continuous recording method that has been used all the way back to when sounds were etched on a tin cylinder. Digital recording breaks down sound information into bits, although it attempts to simulate the sound of analog recording. Recording engineer David Williams said, "It's quite ironic: We got rid of our analog equipment, replaced it with digital, then spent the next couple of decades trying to get the digital to sound like the analog we got rid of."

Digital methods of recording are much easier and cheaper to make than analog recordings. Recording can be done on computers rather than on huge reel-to-reel tape consoles. Artists can access and use digital sounds easily: drum machines, synthesizers, and keyboard sounds can be brought in through computers so an artist does not even need a band. The digital information is easy to edit, and one can copy the digital recordings over and over again without degradation in quality. Digital files kept in a computer do not wear out, whereas tapes stretch, break, or jam, and records scratch.

By the end of the 1990s, the technology was in place for consumers to record on blank CDs, putting an end to the popularity of cassette tapes. Digital songs could be put on personal computers in a format called MP3, a compressed file that reduced the amount of megabytes needed to store a song. The MPMan F10 is considered the first MP3 portable player, manufactured by Korea's Saehan Information Systems in 1988. It resembled a small bathroom scale. The Rio PMP300 from Diamond Multimedia was introduced a few months later. Because MP3s were stored on computers it gradually became easy for people to trade music via computers, and sites like Napster (founded in 1999) made it possible for music lovers to access each other's music almost instantly via the World Wide Web. This is called peer-to-peer (P2P) sharing. The record industry eventually saw a huge loss of CD sales and began to combat this type of file sharing, which is illegal. Still, album sales remained relatively high through 2000. The Recording Industry Association of America (RIAA) reported CD sales at 722.9 million in 1995, rising to 942.5 million in 2000, and dipping to 705.4 million in 2005. The RIAA campaigned against and successfully closed Napster in 2001, and brought suit against individuals who were illegally sharing music. Napster later returned as a site where listeners could pay to legally download music. But online file-sharing services continued to spring up and public backlash arose against the record industry, which was seen as using excessive measures against those who were sharing the music they loved.

In 2001 Apple introduced the iPod. This portable, personal music player changed the recording industry. The device made it easy to take audio file formats and listen to them anywhere. The device was born from the ingenuity of an inventor, Tony Fadell, who figured out a means to store many gigabytes of data on a tiny hard drive. His invention—a small, portable digital music player—was turned down by RealNetworks Walkman. The device succeeded because it is easy to use. Apple made the interface with the computer simple, and that was key for consumers to buy music online and download it

INTERVIEW

How the Past Shaped the Present

Chris Butler
Songwriter and producer

What do you think it takes to be successful in the recording industry and music business today?

You're back to the original way of being successful. You have to play live and build an audience. The major record labels have recognized the importance of the revenue stream from the live shows, and many have signed new acts to deals that include the label receiving a portion of live show revenue and a cut of merchandise sales. For the most part, history has shown that even the biggest acts in music history have started locally, played many live shows, and built a following before becoming hugely popular. Michael Jackson, Bruce Springsteen, the Beatles, and Jay-Z played thousands of shows in front of live audiences. Elvis Presley built his career up by playing in front of live audiences, wowing the females in the crowd with sex appeal and wiggling hips. These acts all became some of the biggest selling recording acts of all time, but first they needed to connect with an audience and build their followings and get the practice to hone their sound and get a professional act. That's how the Waitresses started—playing locally before becoming a national act.

In this business, it sounds like you have to be tuned into what's popular no matter what career you have. Is that the case?

Anyone in the recording industry has to recognize the connection between the music stars and recording professionals who do the actual engineering. Without the talent, there is no recording industry. Those involved in today's recording of artists keep well-informed of the talent. Top recording studios seek out rising talent and make a reputation by recording popular artists. Studios obviously have an interest in cultivating these relationships and it helps to have an ear and eye for what's popular. What acts have sex appeal? What acts have the hype?

Has "hype" always been an important factor in the recording biz?

Look back at the history of the recording industry and there's always an element of P.T. Barnum. [Barnum is known as an early expert of hyping or promoting his circus shows. "Without promotion, something terrible happens—nothing!" said Barnum. He also said that ambition, energy, industry, and perseverance were indispensable requisites for success in business.] All music acts throughout history needed to invent themselves. You need a look, a style, a unique hook. You have to be able to sell yourself. A lot of artists are good, but they never get heard because they don't know how to hype themselves.

Often, hype and promotion simply build from playing lots of live shows. And the youth have often dictated what's popular. In the 40s, young people enjoyed Bing Crosby and Frank Sinatra, but a generation later young people pushed the big band sound to the background as they favored rock 'n' roll. In a later generation, rap and hip hop music would dominate, all based on the tastes of what young people like.

So keeping up with what the youth market likes is important? I think the record industry may be a bit baffled about what to make of the phenomenon that is *American Idol*. The viewing audience to watch total amateurs compete is huge. Still, labels have been signing the winners. If you're in the recording industry, it makes sense to keep up with what youth are listening to. New music comes out of the youth scene and the streets. Along the way, record labels have had to keep up with these tastes or suffer a potential loss in sales. Sometimes the major labels were slow to see coming trends. Decca, Columbia, and HMV turned down the Beatles. The head of Decca Records reportedly told The Beatles manager: "Groups with guitars are on the way out." Paul Cohen at Decca has the dubious honor of also firing Buddy Holly from Decca, calling him "the biggest no-talent I've ever worked with." The heavy metal band Van Halen had its first demo tape rejected by every major record label. Linkin Park was rejected by every major label.

Throughout recording history, artists have come out of an independent music scene. In the early 1950s, the big five major labels were Columbia, RCA Victor, Decca, Capitol, and Mercury. But many independent labels flourished and grew to become major forces because they were able to spot and foster talent. Berry Gordy was just an assembly worker at Ford Motor Company, but with an $800 loan he was able to start Motown Records in 1959. The independent label went on to release top-selling hits by Stevie Wonder, Marvin Gaye, Diana Ross & The Supremes, and the Jackson Five. It became the most successful label of the decade. Through the 60s many independent labels flourished, including Kama Sutra Records (releasing the Lovin' Spoonful), Sire Records, and Fantasy. The Beatles formed Apple Records in 1968. In 1969 Capricorn and Chrysalis labels were launched. Herb Alpert started the very successful A&M Records.

(continues on next page)

INTERVIEW

How the Past Shaped the Present (continued)

In the world of rap music, Joe and Sylvia Robinson formed Sugar Hill Records in 1974. The label released "Rapper's Delight" by the Sugar Hill Gang in 1979. Rick Rubin started the Def Jam label from his dorm at New York University in the early 80s, and went on to release hit albums by Public Enemy, LL Cool J, and The Beastie Boys.

In the 1990s in the Northwest, the independent label Sub Pop [was] discovering and marketing a new independent rock labeled "grunge." The label signed Pearl Jam and Nirvana. Sub Pop continues to thrive discovering and signing new and talented bands like the Shins.

I keep hearing that there's a real do-it-yourself (DIY) movement now. That seems to be the case, but has the do-it-yourself approach always been a part of this industry?
Yes. The music industry has always thrived on this independent, DIY (do-it-yourself) spirit, and the success of these independents has depended on knowing the music that young people are listening to and staying in touch with the music that is coming up from the streets.

While the youth market has always shaped the recording industry, how has technology shaped the industry?
Looking back through the history of recorded music, technology leads the industry. The quest throughout is to make recordings that the consumer can own and keep with them. As the players and recorded products become more affordable, consumers can make music more a part of their everyday lives.

Music has always become more portable and more personal: qualities that consumers want in their product. Also, as recording media developed, the industry adjusted and had to deal with copyright and ownership questions. When cassette tape and the personal Walkman caught on, labels were concerned as consumers recorded records and listened to them on their personal devices. [In the 80s, the British Phonographic Institute started an anti-copyright campaign with the slogan: "Home taping is killing music."]

From the recording industry reaction to cassette tape recording, you could almost predict that they would take drastic measures to try to stop MP3 file sharing later on. The history of music shows that those who have made the music—the manufacturers and the artists—have always sought ways to prevent the consumer from getting music for nothing.

From the manufacturers' perspective, if you had a copy of music, you should pay for it. From the artist's perspective, if the music were being sold or played by someone who was making a profit from it, the artist should get paid. That's why ASCAP seeks fees from radio stations that play music for commercial gain. In 1940 the radio broadcasters began to boycott all music that was registered to ASCAP so they would not have to pay the fees that would ultimately go to the artists who created the songs. The radio stations relied on more regional music, which did not have a deal with ASCAP. Once ASCAP agreed to set fees lower than it had originally planned, broadcasters and ASCAP came to terms. ASCAP also collects fees from TV and cable, bars, clubs, restaurants, shopping malls, concert halls, and airlines—all who use music to enhance their business. Lately, ASCAP has faced the challenge of collecting from Web radio and other forms of Web use. In the spring of 2009, a federal court ordered YouTube to pay ASCAP $1.6 million in royalties. In 2008 a New York federal judge came up with a formula for large Webcasters like AOL, RealNetworks, and Yahoo to pay songwriters and music publishers for streaming their music.

How has technology affected the music business today?
Technology has upset the business model all along the way. Every innovation from the wax cylinder to the record to radio to the Internet to MP3s has changed how the recording industry does business. The biggest problem with the new Internet technology is that there has been no actual physical product to sell and that depletes the revenue stream to the artist and record labels. The labels are trying to stop illegal sharing of files because under the old models if you wanted a copy of the music you loved you absolutely had to buy it and it was incredibly hard to simply share it. Now with a click of the finger on the Internet you can download music from file-sharing services.

How do you think the record industry's approach of taking legal action against those who have illegally downloaded music has worked?
The recording industry became the Goliath and the music listener became David. The record industry has realized that this aggressive prosecution of music fans is backfiring and RIAA has said that it has stopped filing such suits. Now, the organization is working with Internet providers to battle the biggest offenders. Web services like Limewire continue to provide free file sharing for the masses.

The bottom line again is that there are more music fans than ever and the digital age has helped spark new interest in music. But the new technology has brought about a shift in the way the recording industry does business.

into their portable device. The iTunes store also made it easy to shop for music and the price was affordable. In 2007, Apple launched the iPhone, which combines iPod and phone functions, but also allow for multimedia play and Internet access.

The record industry had been trying to control the sharing of music through Digital Rights Management (DRM). Songs on iTunes were originally sold starting in 2001 with DRM restrictions so the tunes could only be played on iPods, and users could play their DRM-protected music on up to five computers. The DRM protection was designed to prevent piracy—illegal distribution and copying of music. However, Apple stopped selling music restricted by DRM in 2009. A January 2009 Macworld.com article states that even without DRM protection, "passing songs around is music piracy. However, the lack of DRM allows you as the consumer to be the judge of what's right and what's wrong… Putting a song up on a file-sharing service and letting 20 of your friends download it? That's now possible but not exactly ethical." Apple embeds a consumer's iTunes ID into every iTunes music file that is purchased, so it is simple to track who originally bought the file.

Today, Apple sells single songs for about 99 cents each. Some songs sell at 69 cents and some sell for $1.29. Currently, the industry has no clearcut plan on how to stop file-sharing, although its policy of suing music fans for illegal downloads may be garnering more ill will. In June of 2009, a jury ruled that Jammie Thomas-Rasset willfully violated copyright laws for illegally sharing 24 songs by Gloria Estefan, Green Day, and Sheryl Crow, and awarded the recording companies $80,000 per song or a total of $1.92 million. Thomas-Rassert, a mother of four from Minnesota, does not have the means to pay the award, and the Recording Industry Association of America has said that it is willing to negotiate the amount. Throughout recording history, the industry has fought against illegal sharing or use or selling of music. Critics have said that cases like the one against Thomas-Rassert have led to a public backlash against the music industry.

Many music fans take the practice of getting music for free as granted. In an interview in *Billboard* magazine, from June 1, 2009, Hilary Rosen, the judge who presided over the case that shut down Napster, looked back at that period and stated that if RIAA had handled its reaction to shared music differently, things would be different. In the article, she states that RIAA made itself the bad guy, the target for the music-buying public's anger. Rosen then states that the recording industry needs to educate listeners more to the fact that music has value and to work with the public to come up with reasonable solutions. Those pursing a career in this business have to consider how to best use downloadable music files and keep up with the legal implications. Opportunities may develop in how to protect these files, how to charge for them, or how to best use them for publicity purposes.

A Brief Chronology

1857: Édouard-Léon Scott de Martinville invents the phonautograph, a machine to study the pattern of sound waves made on a sheet of paper blackened by the smoke of an oil lamp.

1877: Thomas Alva Edison introduces his audio recording device called the "talking machine." The device records sounds onto cylinders.

1887: Emile Berliner develops a device called the gramophone to record onto flat discs and by 1888, he has a method for reproducing the discs in large numbers.

1889: Coin-in-the-slot facilities open for the public to hear entertainment recordings.

1890: The two competitors in the cylinder player market are Edison's phonograph and graphophone, invented by Chichester Bell and Charles Tainter.

1892: Nikola Tesla demonstrates the first complete radio transmitter and receiver system.

1894: Guglielmo Marconi invents a spark transmitter with an antenna in Bologna, Italy.

1898: Valdemar Poulsen patents the telegraphone, the first successful magnetic recording device.

Early 1900s: Cylinders compete against Berliner's discs, played on the gramophone.

1906: The Victor Talking Machine Company, with rights from Berliner, introduces the Victrola model of gramophone, which becomes so predominant it becomes the generic term of the day for record player.

1909: First official "album" is released: Tchaikovsky's *Nutcracker Suite*.

1914: The American Society of Composers, Authors, and Publishers (ASCAP) is founded.

1917: "Over There" by George M. Cohan becomes World War I hit recording.

1920: KDKA radio, out of Pittsburgh, makes the first commercial broadcast.

1923: Record industry hits a slump because of the popularity of radio. Listeners start getting their music for free and not buying recorded product.

1925: The first electrical recordings are put out by Victor and Columbia.

1927: The first major commercial "talking" picture debuts: *The Jazz Singer* starring Al Jolson.

1933: Wurlitzer becomes one of the main sellers of jukeboxes to taverns and other post-Prohibition venues.

1934: General George Squier comes up with another unique way of disseminating music through a service called Muzak.

1936: The company BASF/EG makes the first *tape* recording of a live concert.

1937: First soundtrack album released by Walt Disney for *Snow White and the Seven Dwarfs*.

1942: Glenn Miller becomes the first artist to sell 1 million records with his hit song "Chattanooga Choo-choo." Bing Crosby records the biggest selling song of all time: "White Christmas."

1946: Clarence Fender designs the first commercially successful electric guitar.

1947: Les Paul makes what is considered the first multitrack recording with the song "Lover (When You're Near Me)," featuring Paul playing eight different electric guitar parts.

1948: Microgroove technology and advances in plastics lead to long-playing records with low surface noise. Columbia introduces the first 33 1/3 rpm, 12-inch microgroove LP.

1949: RCA debuts the 7-inch, 45 rpm record, which became a staple for releasing single songs.

1952: Cleveland radio deejay Alan Freed coins the phrase "rock 'n' roll" for a new form of music based around the electric guitar.

1954: Elvis Presley releases "That's All Right" and a major rock superstar is born.

1959: The first Grammy Awards are presented for best recordings.

1962: Phillips of the Netherlands releases first compact audiocassettes.

mid-1960s: The 8-track tape player appears on the music scene.

1967: First digital tape recorder is invented.

mid-1970s The boom box arrives on the scene and becomes associated with playing music outdoors and on the street, especially hip-hop and rap.

1978: The first entirely digitally recorded popular music album is Ry Cooder's *Bop Till You Drop*.

1979: Introduction of the Sony Walkman.

1980: The first commercial recording on CD is released, Richard Strauss's *Eine Alpensinfonie*.

1981: Abba releases *The Visitors*, claiming to be the first commercial CD rock album.

1982: One of the first albums release on CD is Billy Joel's *52nd Street*; it comes out almost at the same time that Sony introduces its CDP-101 CD player.

1983: Bruce Springsteen's *Born in the U.S.A.* (appropriately enough) gets the honors for first CD manufactured in the United States.

1984: Introduction of CD Walkman.

1988: The MPMan F10 is considered the first MP3 portable player, manufactured by Korea's Saehan Information Systems.

1994: WXYC in Chapel Hill, North Carolina begins broadcasting on the Internet.

1999: The music file-sharing service Napster debuts. The Recording Industry Association of America sues Napster the same year for facilitating piracy.

2001: Apple introduces iTunes for Macintosh computers, and the iPod, a portable digital audio player. The first iPod can hold 1,000 songs. Tony Fadell is the inventor who perfects the technology. His invention had been turned down by RealNetworks and Phillips before he approached Apple. XM Satelllite Radio launches, providing radio via satellite to subscribers.

2002: *American Idol* debuts.

2004: Apple launches the iPod mini.

2005: Pandora Media launches Pandora.com, a site offering free personalized Internet radio.

2007: Apple launches the iPhone.

2009: Apple announces about 225 million iPods have been sold. (source: http://www.afterdawn.com/news/archive/19294.cfm)

Chapter 2

State of the Industry

A recording industry professional traditionally works in a studio specifically designed to capture music (as heard on a CD or MP3, for example) or spoken word (as you might hear in a radio or TV commercial). While the engineers and producers are the professionals who actually record sound, many other professionals are involved in the recording business, including those who make music, those who publicize music, and those who distribute and sell the recorded product. There are related careers in broadcasting for professionals who record music for television, film, and radio, and those who handle the actual broadcasting of sound.

The recording industry right now is adjusting to major changes. At its foundation, the recording industry has been the music business, which has most recently relied on the sales of CDs to generate a profit. But with the invention of downloadable music, the business model began to change. Consumers were suddenly able to share music freely and easily via the Internet. The recording industry has been grappling with how to handle the widespread phenomenon of music downloads and how to best make a profit. As the popularity of this new music format has grown, CD sales have plummeted. Nielsen Co. reported total album sales at 428.4 million units in 2008, down from 500.5 million in 2007 and 942.5 million in 2000.

PricewaterhouseCooper, one of the world's largest professional services firms, predicts a contraction of 4.4 percent annually, from $9 billion in 2008 to $7.2 billion in 2013 for the recorded music business. While physically distributed music will decline from $6.2

billion in 2008 to just $2.1 billion in 2013, digital distribution will see a compound annual increase of 12.5 percent to $5.1 billion in 2013. PricewaterhouseCooper also forecasts that digital music will overtake physical music by 2011.

Those in the business have faced many questions about how to best control the illegal sharing of music, how to sell these digital audio files, and how to expand business to accommodate for the drop in CD sales. Opportunities have come through different channels: placing more music in films, TV shows, and commercials; incorporating music in computer and console games; and making music available for cell phone applications. Professionals have had to think more creatively and diversify their skills to succeed.

Current Salaries and Wages

According to SimplyHired.com, the average salary in the recording industry is $45,000, but the range of wages is very diverse depending on the position. According to the Bureau of Labor Statistics, the demand for positions in the recording industry is expected to grow about as fast as the average for all positions through 2014. Though competition is expected to be strong, many positions will open up from turnover and expanded growth in the recording industry itself. (See Chapter 3 for a review of some of the integral positions in this field and the latest earnings statistics.)

Hours and Working Conditions

If you have never been in a professional recording studio, you should know that most share similar qualities. They are clean, temperature-controlled environments designed to protect expensive audio equipment. They can be surprisingly quiet in most rooms because recording engineers do not want to record ambient, or outside, noises when they are in session. Most have comfortable couches and a lounging area where artists can take a break, and most come equipped with kitchens so artists can easily stop for food and drink.

Typically, studios have at least three workrooms. One is the room where music is created, often referred to as the "live room." This is where the musicians set up and play and sing into microphones. This is also the room that studio architects must devote the most time to in order to achieve ideal acoustic conditions. The second room is called the control room. This is where the engineer operates the mixing console, computers, and multitrack recorder. The third room is called the machine room. It is where noisier equipment is stored so it does not disrupt a recording session. Many recording studios also have a vocal booth, a small room designed especially for voice recording. A vocal booth is a type of isolation booth, which keeps out foreign sounds. Studios may also have a room dedicated to editing and mixing.

Those stepping into a recording industry career should realize that a lot of the work is project oriented. This means that when there is a project, the hours can be very long to meet deadlines. However, it also means that there can be long stretches without work in between projects.

A typical project day for a recording industry professional begins with the opening of the studio between 8 and 9 A.M. to get ready for the day's sessions. The studio manager will review what clients are coming in to record at what time. He or she will make sure that the recording technicians prepare each room in advance so each facility is ready to go when the clients arrive. This may mean setting up microphones, amplifiers, or other musical equipment. Along with a recording engineer, the technicians run tests to make sure that all equipment is functioning correctly. They also check to see that everything is looking neat and clean, the garbage is thrown out, and there is adequate food and drink on hand in the kitchen to keep clients fueled throughout the recording process.

Often musicians will not come into a recording session until mid-morning, so technicians tend to have time to get equipment ready and room conditions in top shape. When the client arrives, the recording engineers and possibly the assistant engineers and technicians will review with the client what they hope to achieve that day. If the client is a musical act with a producer, the producer may set the agenda for what needs to be accomplished. Before actual recording starts, engineers will typically create a channel list, which indicates what audio information is being recorded on each specific channel on the mixing board in the control room. For example, the lead vocal may be on channel one, the guitar on channel two, the bass on channel three, and so on. With everything clearly noted, engineers can easily bring up volumes and add effects on the different audio inputs as they record. Meanwhile, technicians may be in the live room with musicians, assuring that microphones are properly connected and placed so they are picking up the audio. Engineers and assistants may discuss what types of microphones are best for each sonic element being recorded, be it drums, piano, voice, or another component.

With all microphones in place, the engineer checks levels, effects, and overall sound to make sure everything is right before hitting the record button. Some of the technical audio elements to check are the EQ, phase difference between mics, and loudness so levels are not going into the red. (See Chapter 5, "Talk Like a Pro", for specific definitions.) Also, if a group is recording, everyone will have to be able to hear each other in the headphones, so an engineer will check that there is a good "headphone mix" for all recording.

It can easily take two to two-and-a-half hours simply to get everything set up, sound checked, and functioning properly before the actual recording starts. The engineer gives a signal and the artist will perform, sing, play music, read lines—depending on what the project is. Typically, if a band is being recorded live in the room, they will play the songs through a few times and then the engineer will have the band come into the control room to listen. Sometimes, an engineer will want to focus on the rhythm track first and get bass and drums perfect. That is often the foundation, and then guitar, vocals, and other instruments can be layered on top of that.

Each time an act records is called a "take," and the engineer, producer, and musical act can review which take is best and use that for the final. Sometimes, in the final mix, an engineer will use bits from different takes to piece together the perfect final audio piece. After the act has recorded everything for the day and they pack up and leave, the assistant typically packs away the microphones, carefully coils up the microphone cables, and puts away the microphone stands.

Another day may be devoted to mixing the recording—taking all the recorded elements, listening to them, and then bringing them together for a final mix. Often a studio will have a room or rooms dedicated specifically to this purpose. Nowadays, it is typical to do the mix in a room with a computer equipped with Pro Tools software and good speakers to hear everything perfectly. Along the way, the mixing engineer adjusts levels and adds in effects. When final mixes are ready, he or she will make copies onto a CD, which will be delivered to the client for review. The producer and musician may have feedback on a project, and the engineer will have to go back and adjust the mix.

Often projects are due by a certain deadline, and recording professionals will stay in the studio beyond the normal workday. While mixing and recording represent the bulk of a typical workday, some portions of the day may be devoted to reviewing audio files and seeing what can be discarded or what has to be carefully stored and backed up; billing clients; contacting potential clients; considering marketing and advertising strategies; and organizing, cleaning, and testing equipment.

Professionals involved in recording video game audio work in similar conditions as recording engineers. Film sound technicians may work mixing sound in a studio, but they also get to go out on location to set up microphones, hold microphones, and operate recording equipment. Television, radio, and film audio pros may work with directors, announcers, actors, and many others who are involved in creating the final show or movie. Those on the broadcast side of audio may work indoors in comfortable, air-conditioned studios for TV and radio, adjusting levels and helping capture audio for broadcast. Finally, some audio projects take engineers and technicians out of the studio. Mixing sound at a concert, for example, may take them to a huge venue full of people and force them to deal with

Fast Facts

The Top Three Sellers of 2008

Sales may be down, but the CD is far from dead. In fact, the top three CDs of 2008 (according to Nielsen Sound-Scan) represent the genres of rap, rock, and country:

1. Lil Wayne *Tha Carter III*; 2.87 million
2. Coldplay *Viva la Vida* or *Death and All His Friends*; 2.14 million
3. Taylor Swift *Fearless*; 2.11 million

Even though these represent big sales numbers, this is the first year the number-one record sold fewer than 3 million copies since Nielsen SoundScan began tracking sales in 1991. While sales from digital music such as iTunes are rising dramatically each year, the profits are far less compared to those formerly generated by physical sales. Veterans in the music industry are struggling to adjust to the model where CD sales are not as popular as digital downloads.

dozens more behind the scenes. Some engineers will go on location with portable gear to record in-store performances or college lectures. Such engineers often work nights, when live performances often take place.

The Changing Tune of the Music Business

The recording industry as we know it is in a state of change, and as the overall business changes, some new growing pains can be expected. On the downside, CDs, which account for a huge percent of recording industry profits, have been on a downward sales trend. They dipped about 16 percent in 2008 compared to 2007, according to Nielsen SoundScan. Since 2000, CD sales overall have plummeted about 45 percent.

Music stores have been especially hard hit, and many large chains have been forced to scale back or close shop. Retail giant Tower Records closed down all its retail stores by 2006, and Virgin MegaStores shuttered all its megastores in the United States by 2009. Big-box retail stores such Target, Walmart, and Best Buy have reduced the floor space formerly devoted to selling CDs.

The good news is that more music listeners are changing their habits and buying music in digital form. Sales of digital albums rose 27 percent from 2007 to 2008. Tower Records, although scaled back, maintains an online presence and sells music via the Internet. The spread of high-speed broadband Internet has made it easy for consumers to download their favorite music. Many in the industry now have to make dramatic shifts as the business evolves, figuring out ways to sell and produce digital music files rather than hands-on product. The new industry landscape has forced major labels to scale back and reduce staff. So those entering the field have to keep an eye for opportunities in cutting-edge and growth areas, such as digital downloads, phone applications, and licensing music for television and film.

The biggest player in the digital music business is Apple's iTunes. Apple, under the leadership of Steve Jobs, became the technological innovator in this field. Apple made songs readily available to the public for 99 cents each via iTunes, and the company created a consumer-friendly way for the public to listen to the songs via its own product—the iPod. Introduced on October 23, 2001, the iPod is the world's most popular portable digital music player. The device lets users easily transfer music that they have downloaded from the computer to their iPod, so they can take the tunes with them wherever they go. Apple went on to create iPods capable of displaying both photos and video. In a short eight years, the iPod products have expanded to include the iPhone and iPod Touch. The iPod Touch gives the user access to the Web though a wireless connection. This latest sophisticated technology lets the user instantly download music, as well as games, applications, movies, and TV shows, all for a price and all providing revenue streams for Apple and the labels that distribute and produce the music.

Another popular format for downloadable music is the MP3. In 1999, the independent record company SubPop (which discovered the band Nirvana) became the first to distribute music using this technology, which compresses the sound of digital audio files by cutting details out of the audio information without disrupting how the music sounds to the average listener. Like iTunes, MP3.com also sells digital music over the Internet. According to the *New York Times*, though, Apple commands an estimated 75 percent of digital music sales and 80 percent of digital audio player sales. Apple popularized the iPod players, and the popularity of those players drove the sales up for iTunes. Anyone in the industry today has to be aware of how iTunes has created this model for success. Many seek jobs supporting this technology or positions in firms that are developing similar digital technology. Those with technical savvy may be finding opportunities with related music sites such at NexTune, eMusic, and Samsung Media Studios.

Critics of the recording industry say that major labels made a big mistake by fighting against digital technology as it was first introduced. Instead of embracing the new technological wave and figuring out how best to take advantage of it, music labels found themselves playing catch up as a company like Apple gained a huge hold on the digital download business, and alienating music fans in the process. Those working at record labels have to be savvy enough to know that deals made with iTunes are increasing the revenue stream to the label. Recent history shows that the career wave of the future will be focused on selling digital downloads and using them to promote music rather than on CD sales.

The industry was and still is concerned with those who are illegally downloading or sharing music, a process that is much easier with songs that are in the electronic format of MP3s. Big labels blame illegal file-sharing services for billions of dollars in losses. Peer-to-peer (or P2P) networks like Gnutella, Morpheus, Kazaa, and

Limewire have allowed music fans to upload and share music with one another for free. According to 2009 data from Big Champagne, a company that tracks music downloading, more than one billion files are shared each month over P2P networks.

The Recording Industry Association of America (RIAA), which represents Vivendi SA's Universal Music Group, Sony Corp's Sony BMG Music Entertainment, EMI Group, Ltd., and Warner Music Group, has taken the position that every recording of a song should create revenue for those who make the music. For five years, the RIAA employed a group called MediaSentry to find those who were uploading vast amounts of music. However, at the beginning of 2009, the RIAA dumped the service because of the public backlash. Many critics believe that the RIAA has become the enemy in the eyes of the music consumer by actively seeking to prosecute individuals sharing music files. For professionals in the recording industry, the question is how to best use downloadable music. Can labels generate a profit selling downloadable music files at a low price point? Also, those in the recording industry are learning from recent history that suing the small music consumer may not be the best approach to addressing illegal file sharing. Those in the field today have to think of creative solutions to this problem.

For professionals in the recording industry, file sharing at this time has meant a reduction in opportunities as it has led to decreased revenues for record labels, and artists. With more files shared, fewer CDs and other recorded matter have been bought. The job gains come from those who are seeing how to best use the new technology. A technology expert who knows how to make music-related applications for the iPhone and cell phones may be in great demand because he or she is pioneering the use of emerging technology on a product that is hugely popular. As Al Houghton at Dubway studios points out, his recording studio found opportunities by recording the live concerts presented by Apple and iTunes in their store. Dubway saw where the opportunities were arising because of the emerging technology and took advantage of that. The advent of digital recording, editing, and broadcasting has greatly changed the work of sound engineers, broadcast technicians, and radio operators. Software on desktop computers has replaced specialized electronic equipment in many recording and editing functions. This transition has forced technicians to learn computer networking and software skills.

To control piracy or the illegal reproduction and selling of music, some record labels have used digital rights management (DRM) technologies. DRM techniques use encryption to prevent illegal access and reproduction. Encryption might limit how many times a song can be played or on what device it can be played on. But since Apple announced that all iTunes would be free of DRM, it seems that the future use of encryption and DRM is uncertain.

While the industry is still trying to pursue legal measures against those who illegally download to combat its losses, it has been learning from its mistakes and changing tack. Labels have now been trying to do all they can to make digital music affordable and easily available to consumers. For example, record labels are teaming up with cell phone providers and broadband Internet companies to offer unlimited "free" music downloads. The trick is, the music is not really free. The customer is paying a bit extra when buying the phone or Internet service in order to have the ability to download millions of songs. For a $1.38 flat tax on cable service on the Isle of Man (located in the Irish Sea and inhabited by about 80,000 people), users download as much music as they want without an extra charge. This is a model that companies are looking at to generate more income in the recording industry as a whole. Nokia also offers "Comes With Music" phones in some markets around the globe, but the *free* music downloads it offers are in reality included as built-in fees consumers must pay for the monthly service. PricewaterhouseCoopers (PwC) predicts that digital music sold over mobile phones will actually decrease in the future, from $868 million in 2008 to $720 million by 2013. Bill Coburn, partner at PwC, attributed the expected decrease to an economic slowdown, shifting consumer behavior, and new ad-support revenue models.

Cell phones have had a major impact on the music industry. The latest sophisticated models let users download tunes right into their phones. In six months at the end of 2008, Apple reported the downloading of more than 300 million iPhone applications. Music fans also want ringtones that play their favorite riffs—and these all come at a cost for the consumer. In terms of careers, this means more growth for those with the technical knowhow to create phone applications, marketers who help sell the devices, and ultimately, the recording engineers and musicians who provide the content that consumers play on these phones.

As the entire music industry switches more to downloadable digital music as a revenue stream, they have found additional income in new MP4 technology, the video version of the MP3. For a price, Beyoncé-lovers can download her latest video directly into a phone or a video-equipped iPod. Career-seekers may find opportunities at

On the Cutting Edge

Rebirth of Vinyl

The RIAA reported that in 2007 sales of new extended play (EP) and long play (LP) vinyl records were up 36.6 percent from the year before. Audio lovers claim that the sound quality of vinyl is far superior to that of CDs and MP3s. Audio on vinyl cannot be compressed to the extremes that it can be on CDs and MP3s. Some industry professionals say that music enthusiasts want MP3s for when they are out and vinyl for when they are listening at home. With the vinyl record, music lovers can still enjoy the big cover art. In 2008, Elvis Costello first released his album *Momofuku* only on vinyl and as a digital download. CNET speculated in March 2008 that by releasing on vinyl, Elvis was attempting to fight piracy to a degree. It is much harder to make MP3s from vinyl. Josh Madell, the co-owner of the independent New York City record store Other Music, has said that vinyl and downloads might replace the CD because he's noticed an increase in those who are buying vinyl over CDs. This is a small but growing trend worth keeping your eye on, and may influence professionals who work at both independent and major labels as they make manufacturing and marketing decisions on new music.

record labels, coordinating the production of MP4 files and negotiating their sale through iTunes. The MP4 has also given new life to the video director who now can reach a wider audience through this downloadable technology.

Influential producer and co-head of Columbia Records, Rick Rubin, said in a September 2, 2007 article in the *New York Times* that the future of the music industry is in a subscription model whereby listeners pay for their music in a similar way that they pay for cable television. He envisions a world where the music fan pays about $20 to have full access to a virtual, digital library of music. The listener could access the library through his or her iPod, cell phone, computer, television, or even a special car radio. This is the type of forward thinking those in the industry have to consider: career opportunities follow the emerging technologies, and those who understand consumer demand and the new methods of distribution can find opportunities in those areas. Rubin's idea is an innovative way of looking at how to generate income, and the industry needs people with similar ideas to adapt to a changing marketplace.

A model like this keeps a revenue stream coming to the record labels and studios, so the traditional careers such as music producer, recording engineer, musician, audio technician, and others can thrive. It also develops a demand for those who are actually creating digital technologies, those who are storing digital files and providing the means for distributing them, and marketing people who may be selling memberships to access digital music rather than marketing individual CDs.

Back to Basics: Live Music Still Pays

Another strong area related to the recording industry has been live concerts. According to *Pollstar*, the touring-industry trade magazine, ticket sales in North America rose 7 percent from 2007 to 2008. Billboard Boxscore also reported worldwide concert industry grosses of approximately $4 billion in 2008.

It's interesting to note that it's not just the rock, rap, and pop music concerts that are selling tickets. In the October 3, 2008 *Wall Street Journal*, Leon Botstein, the president of Bard College, reported "The number of concert venues, summer festivals, performing ensembles and overall performances in classical music and opera has increased exponentially over the last four decades. There are currently nearly 400 professional orchestras in America, according to the League of American Orchestras, while 30 years ago there were 203. There are up to 500 youth orchestras, up from 63 in 1990. The number of orchestra concerts performed annually in the U.S. has risen 24% in the past decade, to 37,000. Ticket-sale income from orchestra performances grew almost 18%, to $608 million, between the 2004-05 and 2005-06 seasons."

While classical music concerts depend on ticket sales to generate most revenue, rock concerts also sell mountains of T-shirts, posters, CDs, and other paraphernalia.

And wherever there are sales, the recording industry wants a part of the action. New major-label contracts with artists called "360" deals give record labels a percent of the artist's income from concerts and merchandise sales. T-shirt sales at concerts alone can generate healthy profits, according to About.com's Music Careers information.

Today, merchandise goes beyond the ordinary cotton T-shirt. Keith Urban is hawking shirts made from recycled plastic bottles. Radiohead has its shirts in children's sizes and offers female fans halter tops. Bands are also selling caps, tote bags, underwear, sunglasses, and temporary tattoos—all emblazoned with their logos and band names. Not only are these items ringing up sales, they are a great form of publicity. With some basic concert T-shirts selling for as much as $55, the profits from merchandise can really add up. Hoodies with a band logo can run as much as $75. Those in music publicity and promotion know that these products help spread awareness of musical acts. Those running the business end support these products to increase a label's bottom line. Graphic artists find opportunities in the design of these items. Unlike CD or tour data, merchandise sales figures are not readily available, since only some acts report those totals with concert grosses as reported in *USA Today* on July 3, 2008. That said, Brandchannel.com reports that Ozzy Osbourne grossed $35 million in concert sales in 2004, and another $15 million directly from merchandise sales.

As live concerts continue to draw fans, experts are needed who can handle live sound mixing and recording. The opportunities range from controlling the sound in huge venues such as arenas and concert hall to small folk clubs. The success of a live concert depends on the sound engineers. The best band in the world is going to sound horrible and perform horribly if the sound is not good. The industry depends on engineers' expertise and those who know their stuff will stay gainfully employed. The techniques to make a live concert sound its best vary according to the type of performance whether it is a rock concert, a solo artist, or a classical symphony.

Recording a live performance can be more stressful than in-studio recording because there is no room for mistakes. A recording engineer cannot ask a band playing before thousands of screaming fans to play something over if he or she does not have the right level or is not getting a signal in a recording channel. Engineers who record live shows have to make sure that everything is perfect beforehand. They have to insist that the band, singer, or orchestra does a sound check so they can make sure all equipment is properly functioning and levels and tones are correct. If an engineer hears a guitar out of tune in a sound check, he or she can tell the guitarist to tune up in advance to ensure it sounds right on the recording. Recording engineers in this environment need the confidence and maturity to tell artists exactly what they need to make sure the sound is right. Stars

Fast Facts

Recording studios are built from top to bottom to produce great sound. The best studios are built by acousticians who understand the properties of sound and how to construct rooms that provide optimal sound. The professional studios record acts using the best microphones, positioned in ways to effectively capture sounds. Most studios provide high-quality amplifiers. Mixing consoles or sound boards allow producers and engineers to mix and change audio signals that are recorded through different inputs. The engineers can control variables such as loudness and EQ, which is a measurement of the high, lows, and mid-range frequencies. The expertise of a professional studio ensures that background noise is limited, levels are never too loud, and desired effects such as reverb or distortion are easily added in. From the mixing console sounds are fed into a multitrack recorder, probably with 24-track capability at today's pro-studio. Although it does not take more tracks to produce great sounds. The Beatles' producer George Martin recorded and mixed their hit records using an eight-track device.

from Justin Timberlake to Bob Dylan are willing to check equipment and microphone levels with the sound people because they know how much is at stake for getting it right. And they will respect the direction of a sound person who is knowledgeable about getting good sound.

Producing Music in the Modern World

As the business model for major labels is shifting, so is the industry for all those involved in various aspects of the music business, from the performers to the recording studios to those who market and promote the music.

Recording studios have seen a dramatic shift in business, not just because of the swing from CDs to digital sales but as a result of the rise of advanced home studios. Sophisticated computer programs have made it easier for more people to record and "engineer" their own recordings. Some artists are finding that they do not need access to an expensive, the state-of-the-art studio, but can achieve some brilliant results in just a basement or bedroom home studio. Once the artist has made the investment in the equipment, a home studio can be cost effective, since studio time costs a lot and is often deducted by the label from the artist's contracted payment. Even major acts, like the rock band the Eels and Moby, have home-produced music that sells.

While home computers can now produce sounds that are fuller, richer, and more complex than was possible years ago, musical tastes are shifting as well. Music that sounds home-generated is an aesthetic that many listeners now enjoy, and it does not always require sophisticated gear. The rapper Aesop Rock produced his first few albums using a turntable, a microphone, a sampling keyboard, and a couple instruments. He recorded it all into his computer using a Pro Tools setup. Pro Tools combines software and related hardware to record, edit, mix, and master through a Mac or PC computer.

There are many software packages on the market today that can convert a home computer into a mini recording studio. In addition to Pro Tools, there are the programs Garageband, Ecasound, and Audacity. Programs from Audacity are free to download.

The deejay Moby has said that by recording at home he does not have to worry about others showing up, and he can be a total egomaniacal, crazy dictator of his own sound, the *New York Times* reported in 2005.

Creatively, however, the home producer may miss out on feedback from an engineer or even other musicians. The work can be insular and lonely. Many musicians do not want to work as their own technician, producer, and engineer. They would rather have others do the work so they can focus entirely on the creative aspects of their art. When the artist pays a studio to record, he or she can feel more compelled to perform and have the sound and performance just right. Other people can be a good sounding board to help refine ideas. Creative friction can be a good thing.

Setting Up and Maintaining the Modern Studio

For those who run the studios (and those who want to operate pro-sounding home studios), the price for essential gear has dropped in certain areas. For example, high-quality microphones manufactured by Busman Audio and Cascade Microphones are much more affordable than they once were. Also, digital live consoles have improved, boosting the sound quality at live performances.

Although digital recording is a modern method that allows people to easily record and mix on computers, analog recording is a service that most studios still offer. Audiophiles say that with analog recording, the sound wave form most resembles the sound wave of the original source. Phonograph records or vinyl and magnetic tapes are the means to store the continuous audio waves captured in analog recording. Digital recording breaks down the signal into bits of information. Studios can now easily store recorded information on computer hard drives, while in the old days studio shelves were crammed with spools of magnetic tape.

Traditional studios are not dead, but in today's climate they have had to get creative and often expand the types of services they offer. Some successful studios that originally focused on recording pop, rock, and rap groups have developed business related to television, film, and advertising. Producer Butch Vig, in an interview in *Prosound News*, says that many TV shows are interested in cutting-edge music and sound design, which has opened up new opportunities for recording studios that can adapt. Vig says that sometimes studios cannot afford to be so picky and should take work from clientele that may not be so prestigious. Even recording a local high school choir can bring a studio some needed income.

Even as more bands turn to home studios and record labels cut back because of losses, there seems to be no end to the number of people who want to make music. Just surf around MySpace and you will find thousands of people vying to be recognized, appreciated musical artists—from rappers to rockers to country crooners. To reach their goal, many want the best sound possible, and a studio with a track record of producing great sounding albums can still do brisk business. For example, The Clubhouse in Rhinebeck, New York, was booked with artists throughout 2008, and it helped to have artists like Natalie Merchant and Rusted Root as customers, as reported in industry publication *prosoundnews.com*.

Producers who build a track record in popular music will always be in demand. Some of today's top producers are Timbaland (he has produced Nelly Furtado, Justin Timberlake, and the Pussycat Dolls), Rick Rubin (producer of Red Hot Chili Peppers and the last Johnny Cash albums), and Butch Vig (producer of Nirvana and Smashing Pumpkins). But even a studio with a strong musician client base may have to look beyond its core business. The Clubhouse is looking into working more on film soundtracks.

Music Publishing or Perishing

Because diversifying is an avenue to employment for newcomers to the industry and greater profit for those already involved, recording industry jobs now often include involvement in music publishing. In fact, many music producers are also music publishers. *Forbes* magazine reported in the beginning of 2009 that even though CD sales numbers keep slipping, music publishers might still reap a profit. Publishers are in the business of promoting songs, getting deals for their use, and collecting publishing royalties. They collect money on songs that are licensed from them for movies, TV, and advertising. Traditionally, publishing royalties are split 50-50, with half for the publisher and half for the songwriter.

Publishers work with major performance and broadcast rights organizations—ASCAP, BMI, and SESAC. These groups collect money when a song is broadcast, performed in public, or played on a jukebox. Those who use the music pay a fee according to how they are using it. For example, a commercial radio station will pay ASCAP an annual license fee so it can play music, and the fee is based on how big the radio station is. So anytime you hear Bruce Springsteen or Madonna or Coldplay on the radio, the composer and the publisher get paid a fee by the radio station. Cell phone service providers like Verizon are now also paying broadcast rights organizations for usage of music as cellphone ringtones.

Some songs seem to remain eternally popular and bring in a huge revenue stream. The 1967 song "Happy Together" by the Turtles reportedly generates about a quarter million dollars a year in licensing fees. Publishers have even found greeting cards a source of income. Many card manufacturers now insert a chip in the card, which then plays a portion of a song when opened. Publishers have struggled to get income from Internet use of songs, and now some Internet radio stations and online music providers are paying publishers a percentage of overall revenue. Those seeking a career in publishing or as a musician/composer have to be aware of all the latest ways revenue can be generated through broadcast and usage roylaties.

While some artists retain all their publishing rights, others think that publishers can help promote their work and generate even more income. Many top publishers are so well connected in the entertainment industry that they know how to strike lucrative deals for the artists they work with. In the history of music, though, the relationships between artists and publishers have ranged from very positive collaborations to acrimonious struggles for control. In 1964, the Beach Boys complained that their publisher, their father Murry Wilson, sold off the rights to their music for a song, so to speak. Artists such as Laura Nyro and Jimmy Webb, however, reportedly enjoyed their relationships with their publishers and were able to focus more on their music as a result. Little known or unknown songwriters may even be able to make a deal with a music publisher, especially if the publisher sees potential for a song being used in a movie or TV show. Or a publisher might regard a song as a potential hit for one of the established artists they represent. All said, publishing today is one of the shining points in the recording industry and a truly dependable source of revenue.

As outlets in the media have grown, music usage has expanded. Movies, especially hip, new independent films, often want the most cutting edge songs to grace their soundtracks. Securing a spot on the soundtrack for a popular movie can propel an unknown songwriter into the limelight, and onto the music charts. Fame came to the artist Kimya Dawson in just that way when her music was featured in the hit independent movie *Juno*. While she was gaining attention as an independent artist, the popularity of the movie gave her a wave of media attention and introduced her music to many new listeners. The soundtrack to the movie topped Billboard's Digital Albums chart and reached number 8 on the Billboard 200 in the first week of the soundtrack's release.

Promotion on the Cutting Edge

Even though CD sales have been in a slump, the recording industry does not exist without the sale of recordings, and sales do not happen without advertising and promotion. While songs by established artists can receive wide attention upon release, many hit songs and groups start at a grassroots level. Early in the music business, buzz around a song might start at one radio station and spread to others, generating record sales as a result. While that still happens today, the Internet has become one of the best ways for artists to gain fans and generate attention for their music. From U2 and Beyoncé to a one-man kazoo band, every musician today needs a Web page, and most benefit from having a MySpace page or Facebook page as well. MySpace, established in 2003, has become the networking site to go to for bands to post songs and information about themselves and then connect with music fans and professionals in the industry. Recording studios, record labels, radio stations, and marketing firms have all established MySpace presences.

MySpace works on the principal of linking a user to like-minded individuals. If you are in a band, for example, you connect with other bands and people you like, who then display a link to your music on their page. Once you start to link with others, more people discover you and become your virtual "friends." In time, links to your band's site can show up on hundreds or thousands of Web sites. Those numbers add up to amazing advertising, which lead to more product sales. MySpace even has a feature that allows users to download your music, paying a small fee for each song.

Justin Vernon, who goes by the name Bon Iver, is a great example of the power of the Internet and MySpace when it comes to marketing. He is also a true do-it-yourself artist. In 2006, Vernon broke up with his longtime band and girlfriend and holed up in his parents' cabin in Wisconsin to recuperate from a bout of mononucleosis and write some new music. Using a computer with recording software, a guitar, and a few drums, he recorded some very quiet, personal, emotionally charged songs that he posted on MySpace under the name Bon Iver (a corruption of the French phrase *bon hiver*, or "good winter"). The songs caught on fast with music fans, and Vernon generated a lot of buzz on many of the independent music blogs. By the end of 2008, the album he had made of these songs, titled *For Emma, Forever Ago*, sold about 87,000 copies. Vernon has gone on to playing sold-out shows and having an appearance on *The David Letterman Show*—all of this starting by posting a few songs on MySpace.

The Future of Radio in the Age of the Internet

Although the Internet is definitely one of the most important tools artists and labels have today for promoting music, radio airplay remains a major way to push sales in the record industry. For those labels with major artists, radio still provides widespread listenership. Most stations play the biggest acts—the Black-Eyed Peas, Jay-Z, Eminem, and Kanye West. Critics complain that more and more radio sounds the same as a result. Also, over the years, businesses like Clear Channel have bought up radio stations and made them

INTERVIEW

Innovation, Flexibility, and Risk-Taking Are Keys to Survival

Al Houghton
Owner, Dubway Studios, New York City

When VH1 asked you about branching out to make live recordings in their offices, how did you approach the novel work?
We didn't totally know how to do it, and we didn't have all the right gear, but we spent a little money renting some gear, making sure we knew what we were doing, and doing some research beforehand. One of the important parts of the research for something like that is to talk to the people who you're going to be working with and find out what they need and what they expect—so when you walk in there you're going to give them ultimately what they need.

How did the recording job go?
We sent a couple engineers to VH1 with a DAT (digital audio tape) recorder and a couple microphones. As they recorded more shows for VH1, Dubway's team improved their technique. The performances, which started out as simple acoustic shows with a couple guitars, also expanded to big bands, requiring much more elaborate recording. After doing this work for VH1, Dubway had established a name for itself in live recording, so when Apple was looking to record live performances in their store, the company turned to us.

Why did Apple want to record live performances at their store?
For Apple and the music labels, the inspiration of recording live shows in the stores was a winning idea. Apple would get exclusive rights to sell the digital recording of the live performances. Plus, customers would be drawn to the store for performances and some of the shows would gain publicity in the media. The artist would have a concert that would promote their work and give them extra attention on iTunes. We had no idea how popular this would be, but this became regular work for us.

Has recording the live in-store performances for Apple led to more work?
Once Dubway became Apple's go-to team for live recording in New York City and perfected this type of recording, Apple turned to us to

get live recordings of artists performing at a music festival in Miami, Florida. The company hired one of Dubway's engineers to lead the project. Apple flew him to the event and hired the engineer support staff to help out. Once the live shows were recorded, Dubway took the recordings back to the studio and mixed them and added in any additional effects or other elements.

It seems that you've jumped at different types of opportunities as they came along, even if you didn't have all the background needed. Is that one of the keys to succeeding in the recording industry? Being diverse and getting as much different experience as possible?

Taking on different types of recording jobs is essential to survive in today's recording industry. All people entering this field should take the same attitude and approach to the business. The more different stuff you can do, the better. So make yourself available to do anything. Don't say no. If someone asks you if you can do sound at a club, but you don't usually do sound—if you think you can handle it, and you know you won't make a mess of it, then you should do it. You learn by doing different things. You may learn something technically by going there. You may meet different people. If you go into different environments like that, you run into a whole bunch of different people who may overlap with what you do. This is how you build new skills and new opportunities. The bottom line is to try and do as many different things as you can because you may find that you like the other thing more than the first thing you set out to do. Or you'll run into someone who will be an avenue into other work that you didn't expect.

Does having and knowing the latest technology play a role in getting more work for your studio?

Dubway Studios in New York has been getting more and more work doing audio production on television shows, and having the latest, cutting edge technology definitely plays a role. For example, most television production companies that I deal with want to know if the studio has a Dolby LM 100 Broadcast Loudness Meter. Broadcast specifications for TV are very precise. All shows must meet specified volume standards so there is a consistency among shows. The LM 100 is the meter that TV production teams rely on to measure the volume of television audio. The meter, which is an expensive piece of equipment, tells the production company that you're serious about getting the right levels, and you can document that you're actually doing it. Having the right equipment like that helps Dubway secure new business.

(continues on next page)

INTERVIEW

Innovation, Flexibility, and Risk-Taking Are Keys to Survival (continued)

Sometimes, it is not the newest, state-of-the-art devices that attract clients. Certain artists and producers want equipment that is high quality but not widely available any more. For example, some producers and singers like the sound of a classic, old microphone called the Neumann U47, which was the preferred microphone of Beatles producer George Martin. Because these microphones are not very common, a studio that offers the use of one is providing some extra cachet to discriminating singers and producers.

more into cookie-cutter copies of each other. Music playlists at Clear Channel stations (more than 1,200 nationwide) can be remarkably similar.

For those in the industry, this arrangement can be profitable. But for music lovers and those trying to introduce new artists, the trend toward homogenization can be a frustrating cement wall. So while it poses a challenge to musicians and recording studios who are eager to have new artists heard, the big companies like Clear Channel still provide opportunities to broadcast technicians, sales people, marketers, deejays, and others.

Again, the Internet has provided an answer for those looking for more diverse music. Independent radio stations have opened on the Internet for very little cost. They are not beholden to major labels, and they do not follow the dictates of a major broadcasting parent company such as Clear Channel. Nationally, radio listenership has risen from 229 million weekly listeners in 2004 to 235 million in 2008, according to Arbitron. However, a December 5, 2008, article in the *New York Times* showed that the amount of time 18- to 24-year-olds spent listening to radio from 1998 to 2007 had dropped by 18 percent. In terms of how this affects careers in the recording industry, there are certainly fewer radio stations than 20 years ago and fewer opportunities in traditional radio broadcast.

However, traditional radio listeners and potential listeners may be turning more to the Internet to listen to the types of music they are interested in. According to AccuStream iMedia Reseach via Hypebot, online music radio listenership increased 37.6 percent to 6.67 billion total hours from 2007 to 2008. The Internet allows people to tune into exactly the type of music they want to hear. Pandora, an Internet-based "radio" service, asks listeners to fill out a questionnaire about their musical tastes and then tailors a "radio station" to match exactly what they want to hear. When the iPhone included Pandora as one of its applications, listenership jumped from 20,000 a day to 40,000 a day. Pandora's growing appeal has allowed the station to sell short 15-second commercials, which they sprinkle into their free playlists. For many looking to career opportunities in radio, the true growth may be coming from the Internet, and positions as disc jockeys, marketers, and music programmers may be available at online sites. Also, as more traditional radio stations bolster their online streaming capabilities, those in the field may find increased listenership through that avenue. More listeners can generate more advertisers. So the traditional broadcast stations are seeing the Internet-streaming as a way to increase listenership, which in turn keeps advertisers returning, which then keeps the disc jockeys and broadcast engineers employed.

Another development in the world of radio has come in the form of satellite radio (SR)—the biggest player in the United States is Sirius XM Radio, which resulted from the merger of XM Satellite Radio and SIRIUS Satellite Radio in the summer of 2008. SR works on a subscription basis. Customers pay to hear channels that provide the programming that matches their tastes and interests. Because the signal is broadcast via satellite, listeners can tune in anywhere in the country. Many new cars are equipped with SR receivers so listeners can enjoy their stations wherever they travel. SR, with its groups of niche listenership, has helped some new artists trying to gain exposure. To pull listeners in with this new technology, SR paid out a huge sum to recruit the humorous, raunchy deejay Howard Stern, who has a massive and fiercely loyal following. However, even with a celebrity like Stern aboard, SR has struggled to attract listeners, and as of late 2009, the financial viability of Sirius and XM were uncertain. So those considering a career in radio may find opportunities in satellite radio and should keep a careful eye on how that niche develops—the technology is still very promising, but a business model for satellite radio has yet to be proven.

Finally, while radio still offers portability in car radios and carry-along electronics, the Internet is gaining in that regard as more portable devices allow Wi-Fi access. Many people now own cell phones that provide access to a high-speed Internet connection. Listeners can also take radio shows along with them in the form of podcasts. These are programs designed to be downloaded into an MP3 format and listened to on in iPod or similar device. A tech poll from the radio research firm Jacobs Media reported that the audience for podcasts is up about 87 percent each year among rock radio listeners. Of those polled, about 60 percent own an iPod or other type of portable media player. A podcast is nothing more than a digital audio file, just like any other song or MP3 file on your computer.

Recording for Film and Television

Those embarking on a career in the recording industry have to recognize the significant role that film and television has played in recent years. The Disney Channel launched *High School Musical*, and that show has gone on to become a popular phenomenon. The album generated from that program became the top seller of 2006. *American Idol* has introduced the world to best-selling singers such as Kelly Clarkson and Chris Daughtry. Acts that have their songs played on *Gossip Girl* and *Grey's Anatomy* generate more sales.

Sound recording for film and TV is a very specific art and career specialty. A major motion picture or television program hires a sound editor at its helm to direct all the sound components. The sound editor takes all the music, dialogue, background noise, and sound effects and mixes them together so that it best supports the film. Digital recording is now the norm in motion pictures and television series, but sound effects specialists may use a classic analog

On the Cutting Edge

One recent issue that has united the recording industry and the movie industry has been piracy. The digital age has made it very easy to copy films as well as music and reproduce and illegally share or sell the art. With losses over piracy mounting, both industries have been devoting resources to developing sophisticated means of encrypting their products. Encrypting puts a hidden code into a product so it cannot be reproduced illegally.

Nagra tape recorder. The analog Nagra was the recording tool of choice for most films but stopped being used as digital recording took over. They are still especially good for recording extreme dynamic range, such as sounds like gunshots and explosions. The film and television industry relics on specialists who know how to hold the boom microphones and those who record the dialogue and ambient sounds. Sound experts pay close attention to synchronization, a method of timekeeping that ensures images and sound perfectly mesh. Cable and network TV, movies, and even highly produced Web shows are driving the demand for trained recording and sound professionals.

The Gaming World: A New Opportunity for Audio Engineers

If you have seen today's video games, you will know that many are like mini motion pictures, and they often have a professional soundtrack to match. The music in a game like *Halo* enhances the mood and creates a rich ambience. The action hero games can have sweeping majestic theme music and the more cartoonlike games can have amusing scores. Not only are people writing and recording music for the games, they are also recording elaborate sound effects. The professionals who put together all the sounds for these games are called sound designers.

The booming gaming industry has opened up new outlets for publishers as well as they try to license music for computer, console, and Web-based games. Publishers are thinking creatively, finding opportunities in the ring tone and karaoke markets. State-of-the-art computer games have also created many positions for sound designers, composers, sound effects specialists, and the recording engineers and technicians who record the sounds and music created by these professionals. Compared to the overall recording industry, the gaming industry is red hot, and that is why many of those who are involved in recording and music-related careers are taking advantage of compatible opportunities in this area. According to NPD Group, video game sales were about $2 billion in 2008, which is more than double from the year before.

Ken Kato studied digital audio recording in college and wound up designing sounds for games made by Microsoft. In addition to getting appropriate music and voice actors, Kato often goes to different locations to record sounds. He has recorded racetracks and street sounds from around the world. To get the squishing and crunching sounds used in some fight scenes, Kato recorded himself stabbing, smashing, breaking, and hitting various fruits, vegetables, and meats. To get a great monstrous growl for a character, he recorded his tiny toy fox terrier and pitched down her growl until it became a deep threatening rumble. The art of sound design has become so precise, requiring distinct programs and technology, that colleges offer specific courses on how to master it.

The popular console games *Guitar Hero* and *Rock Band* for PlayStation 2 have also opened up opportunity for the recording industry as another outlet to license music and promote bands. Some popular bands, such as Aerosmith and Metallica, have stand-alone versions of the game. Kai Huang, the president of RedOctane.com, the official *Guitar Hero* store and publisher, said in *USA Today* that Aerosmith made more from sales of *Guitar Hero: Aerosmith* than from sales of its last two albums combined. Being on a *Guitar Hero* game is great publicity and those bands see their CD sales climb after being featured.

Employment Trends in the Recording Industry

Broadcast and sound engineering technicians can expect to see employment growing faster than the average through 2016, according to the BLS. Those who land jobs may be expected to know the latest in digital audio recording and broadcasting. A report from IBISWorld in 2008 showed that the demand for the recording of lectures, meetings, and conferences is on the rise. Many people cannot afford the time or money to attend important industry conferences, but they still want to listen to high-quality podcasts or Webcasts of the various lectures so they can keep up with news, trends, and technology. While some opportunities may be growing, others are expected to contract. Businesses engaged in the manufacture, promotion, and distribution of recordings are expected to hire fewer workers between 2006 and 2016, with a decrease of 12 percent in employment in this area, according to the BLS.

Most opportunities in the recording industry remain in major metropolitan areas where major labels, independent labels, TV and film industries, and musical artists thrive—New York City, Los Angeles Chicago, Seattle, and Atlanta, for example. Los Angeles is the entertainment capital of the United States, so many audio engineers find opportunities with film, television, and record labels there.

Similarly, Seattle is a center for computer game development, and many audio engineers find opportunities with the game designers who are based in the Pacific Northwest.

Independent of trends, however, success in the recording industry takes an ability to adapt and an openness to learn and do new things. For example, to be a successful recording engineer, it pays to be an outgoing freelancer. Opportunities to work for big studios on staff are limited. Engineers today have to build relationships with studios and artists. According to the U.S. Bureau of Labor Statistics (BLS), in 2005 there were 10.3 million independent contractors in the United States, representing about 7.5 percent of the total labor force, and because of shrinking economy with fewer staff positions more and more people have been forced to take freelance positions.

Ethical Issues Affecting the Recording Industry

With the advent of digital technology and the resulting freedom to share and pirate music, several ethical issues have become a focus of industry professionals. The preeminent issue involves audio sharing and copyrights. This goes back to the origins of sharing digital audio. Record labels are confronting and defining what piracy means. For music lovers the question is: "Is it okay to copy digital music files and share them with friends without paying anything to the artist or label?" For the music labels, the question is: "Is it okay to let the music listening public share music free of charge, in the hopes that it will help publicize artists and encourage sales of actual product?" The establishing of various digital copyright laws was an attempt by the industry to stop definitely illegal piracy, but also better define the lines between fans sharing music and the illegal sales and distribution of music.

The second major issue has to do with when artists ask for more than is in their contract. When it comes to professional ethics in the business, one dilemma is the lack of clarity with respect to the exact terms of arrangements between those who record the music and the artists and clients who need the projects recorded. Al Houghton of Dubway Studios says that there is ethical decision making on how much service to provide based on contracted work. Often, a client will hire a studio to do engineering on a project and then ask the engineer to provide a keyboard part or suggestions on the mix and overall sound—duties that would traditionally fall into the producer realm. How much extra is appropriate to ask for? Should those in the recording industry provide more than contracted for without compensation? Houghton believes that terms between clients and studios have to be clearly defined upfront.

The third major issue is who, exactly, owns the material? This is also an issue with artists and producers who need to clearly spell out who owns the material and who is shaping the overall sounds of a project. Many musical projects have been shelved over arguments between artists and producers over ownership and overall creative vision.

The following legislation and pending legislation show some of the copyright issues involved with digital recordings. Several laws already in practice have been created in order to arbitrate the complex ethical arguments born of the digital music economy. A few key pieces of legislation are:

➡ The Audio Home Recording Act (1992) This law made it legal to record at home with digital audio recording devices.

➡ No Electronic Theft (NET Act) (1997) This act provides for criminal prosecution of those who engage in copyright infringement, even when there is no monetary profit or commercial benefit from the infringement.

➡ The Digital Performance Right in Sound Recordings Act (DPRSRA) (1995) This law states that performers and owners of copyrights in sound recording must be compensated and can receive a royalty whenever their songs are used in digital transmission.

➡ The Digital Millennium Copyright Act (1996, 1998) This copyright law criminalizes production and dissemination of technology, devices, or services designed to circumvent Digital Rights Management measures, which control access to copyrights works.

➡ Music Online Competition Act (pending) This proposed legislation seeks to streamline the distribution of music over the Internet, increase competition, and avoid monopolization of the online music industry by the record companies.

➡ Consumer Broadband and Digital Television Protection Act (pending) Designed to protect movies, music, and software against digital piracy, the law would enforce standards to ensure the secure transmission of copyrighted content on the Internet and over the airwaves.

Key Industry Events

Recording industry professionals have several chances to meet throughout the year to network and learn about developments in the industry. Some events include:

Digital Music Forum West/Digital Music Forum East At this trade show, digital music companies showcase their services and products. They also have panel discussions and lectures about the latest technology and trends in the field.   (http://www.digital musicforum.com)

The Grammys Organized by the Recording Academy, this awards show recognizes the best in recorded music each year. (http://www .grammy.com)

The NAMM (National Association of Music Merchants) Show This is the trade show to attend to see the latest in musical instruments and related audio gear. The event features plenty of opportunities to network with industry professionals, as well as courses and tutorials on equipment.   (http://www.namm.org/ thenammshow)

National Recording Merchandisers Convention This is a not-for-profit trade association that serves the music-content-delivery community in a variety of areas including networking, advocacy, information, education, and promotion. The core retail membership consists of music wholesalers and retailers, including brick-and-mortar, online, and mobile music-delivery companies. More than that, membership encompasses distributors, record labels, multimedia suppliers, technology companies, and suppliers of related products and services. Individual professionals and educators in the field of music are also members. The annual convention is touted as the event where industry players come together to make business deals, hear live music, get the latest research, see the most up-to-date technology, showcase new product lines, hammer out solutions to industry issues, and network to find new business partners.   (http://www.narm.com)

South by Southwest Music and Media Conference This major independent music and media conference is held once a year in Austin, Texas, and showcases more than 1,800 musical acts. (http://www.sxsw.com)

Chapter 3

On the Job

The music and recording industry definitely has built a reputation as being a very difficult, competitive place. While it takes drive and determination to succeed, not everyone is a hustler. Most people are in the business because it is a creative and technical field. Ultimately, most people are in recording to make music and produce a quality product. The Grammy-award winning producer/engineer Ed Cherney perhaps described the recording industry best: "Where business, commerce, and art all meet at the same intersection." In other words, the music industry depends on a whole lot of creativity, and there are many ways to earn money from that creative energy.

When you think of jobs in the industry, you may think of only the traditional careers, and many of those still hold true: You can work as engineer in a studio; you can work in public relations for a major label; you can work in a live music venue running the sound board and maybe recording live music; you can work as a radio disc jockey. But the industry is in flux and opportunities are arising off the traditional path.

For example, Starbucks now heavily promotes music. This means that there are careers with that company establishing exclusive deals with artists and handling promotion. Most airlines have extensive music-listening options through the headsets in passenger seats. Professionals behind the scenes program that music. Others find unique opportunities as entrepreneurs, taking advantage of the Internet and its ability to offer streaming music and fast downloads. In early

2000, Pandora Media started Pandora.com as a way to provide listeners with a personalized stream of music based on their tastes. Customers pay a small fee for the wireless plan and Pandora generates revenue with advertisements from companies such as Microsoft, Verizon, and Starbucks.

While it is true that recorded music may be the foundation of this industry, there are many other related recorded projects. Commercial studios may strictly focus on recording voices and other sound elements for commercials and other types of TV and radio production. Books on tape, language programs, and education DVDs and CDs all need to be expertly recorded. Think of interactive kiosks that respond with voice information or even prerecord phone messages. To one level or another, a recording professional assisted in getting the audio right for the project.

Also, keep in mind that the recording industry employs people who are not directly involved in the recording or music aspects of the business. Accountants, graphic designers, lawyers, and other professionals with an interest in the industry but a separate and distinct skill set may find employment. So while you may be working in one aspect of the industry already, you may find another career more suitable to your talents that is still within the recording industry. Also, know that many in the industry work on a freelance basis, as staff positions can be difficult to come by, especially in a down economy. One more point: Often professionals today do not hold just one title—a producer may also be an engineer and promoter. Those with diverse skill sets find they have more employment opportunities, so you may find overlap among the career descriptions as well.

Recording Studio and Recording-Related Careers

These careers are all connected to the actual recording process, and most are occupations in recording studios that actually capture songs and other types of audio so they can be reproduced, played back, and broadcast.

Live Sound Engineer

If you have seen a band at a club, the quality of the sound is the responsibility of the live sound engineer. The engineer controls the sound mix during a live performance, sitting behind a soundboard to adjust levels of vocals, amplifiers, drums, and other equipment. These engineers set up sound equipment on stage for sound checks and break down gear when the show is over. When a band sounds great during a show, it is often because the live engineer did a good job, but they work behind the scenes; they often do not get the recognition for contributing to a performance, but they are instrumental in making a successful event. As with all audio engineers, they simply need to have a keen sense for what sounds good, making sure sound is not too loud, tinny, abrasive, or bass-heavy.

Mastering Engineer

In the recording industry, masterers are the ones who put the final touches and final polishing on a recording. By applying subtle equalization effects, they make sure that the final mix of all songs/tracks that comprise a recording are consistent in terms of volume and tone. They also ensure that a recording is up to industry standards, so it has the right overall sound for radio play and other broadcast. Recording studios may employ a mastering engineer, but many who specialize in mastering work in a facility dedicated to the process.

Multimedia Developer

These specialists bring together diverse media elements to create a coherent whole work. For example, they will combine audio, video, animation, still images, and text to create an interactive educational CD or DVD. These experts create Web sites, CD-ROM games, business presentations, elaborate PowerPoint sales pitches, and informational kiosks. Their end product is usually interactive, meaning they want to make sure their product is user-friendly. They often collaborate with other media specialists to bring the different forms of media together. In the business setting, they may work closely with managers to get flow charts, graphs, and statistics and develop a graphically compelling look. They decide the "storyline" for the product—where does the viewer start, where does the viewer wind up, and does the viewer learn all the necessary information in a logical flow?

Developers are like project managers, juggling budgets and work schedules, and serving as a team leader to make sure all elements come together to create the final product. Knowledge of computers

Everyone
Knows

Basic Education for Recording Engineer, Technician, and Related Jobs

Those interested in a career making actual, physical recordings should have a basic interest in electronics and sound. Knowledge of physics and math and how they relate to sound and sound measurements is invaluable. Because sophisticated equipment is involved that must be maintained, repaired, and operated, potential job applicants are wise to have specific training at a two-year technical or community college, or through a four-year public or private college. Courses need to emphasize recording and broadcast technology, principles of electronics, and computers. Those who are audiophiles with a love of stereo equipment and other related electronic gear may have a leg up getting started in this field.

Hobbyists who build their own electronic devices and kits or operate a "ham," or amateur, radio are building skills that are essential to most of these careers. The experience working with wires, transistors, speakers, and other components and the necessary tools (pliers, wire cutters, soldering guns, etc.) translates to many engineering and tech positions. But nothing provides experience better than real life. So interning at a studio, broadcast station, commercial advertising agency, etc., can give the hands-on lessons needed to enter a full-time career. Also note that many engineers and technicians can advance and keep up with the latest technology through certification programs. For example, the Society of Broadcast Engineers offers certification to those demonstrating competence and experience.

and computer programming is often required, and multimedia pros always stay current with the latest developments in digital technology. Many colleges and universities offer courses in multimedia study that train students in the use of computer programs to create multimedia projects. Courses in graphic arts, film, and writing are usually part of the training. Ultimately, clear communication is key.

These specialists combine audio, video, and print for Web sites, educational CDs, and other interactive projects. They earn a median annual salary of $50,360, according to the Bureau of Labor Statistics. This is a rapidly growing field with a high demand for skilled workers.

Producer

The overall role of the producer is to take a musician's or a band's sound and help make it original yet commercial. Producers have an overall vision for how the recorded music should sound, and they oversee a recording project to make sure the right sound, gets recorded. The producer may be the actual recording engineer as well, or he or she may direct the engineer to achieve the desired results. Producers have to listen closely to the artist's concept to make sure they are making a recording that matches that vision. Sometimes, they play psychologist—encouraging the artist to try different sounds or to soldier on into a late session. Sometimes they help band members get along to make it through a recording. During the recording, the producer has to listen closely to the performance of each player to make sure they are performing their parts correctly and with the right feeling. Producers can be almost like an unseen member in a band. The role entails close collaboration. It can be a matter of personal chemistry to find the ideal match of producer and artist. A label or band may hire a producer and pay him or her for the project, or a producer may work for a percentage of final sales. These professionals typically oversee a budget as well—they keep a project running on deadline so costs do not creep up.

The top music producers like Dr. Dre and Timbaland can earn over a $1 million a year because they have a track record of producing hit albums, but there are a wide range of producers. On the lower end of the pay scale, producers can earn about $20,000 a year, according to PayScale.com.

Recording Engineer

A recording engineer is the technical master who knows exactly how to capture the sounds and music an artist makes, and then he or she mixes the sounds to create the perfect overall recording. The engineer works in a studio specifically designed with the right acoustics so sound can be best recorded. Engineers spend most of their time behind a mixing board. Most mixing boards in modern studios have

24 channels. That means there are up to 24 inputs of sound. These are called multitrack recording systems or musical instrument digital interface (MIDI) systems.

The inputs take sound from microphones recording different instruments. For example, one channel may be dedicated to bass; another channel may be for guitar; and one for vocals. A drum kit may require its own channel to capture the sounds of the different drums. By having a microphone recording these different instruments, the engineer can create a better recording and control the parts in the mix. The engineer also knows how to add effects such as more treble or reverb and equalization. In addition, he or she may edit out sound or cut sounds from one area and paste them in somewhere else. When everything is recorded, the engineer then takes the components and puts together a mix for each song or piece.

Engineers have to keep up with all the latest audio technology, especially as it affects digital recording. One of the most recent technological advancements that has had a huge impact on the recording industry is a computer platform called Pro Tools. This digital audio work station for Mac OS X and Microsoft Windows makes it very easy to use a computer to mix and edit recordings and has actually led to the rise of professional home studio recordings. Engineers have to be very technically adept and must understand electronics and computers. Sometimes, fast repairs are required.

The recording engineer may also do most of the roles that the producer does from overseeing the project to soothing band members to get them to perform together. Many schools offer degree programs in recording engineering. College programs give candidates the chance to work with the required technology and computers, as well as the opportunity to record acts. Schools also offer internships at established recording studios so budding engineers can get hands-on practice.

According to SchoolsintheUSA.com, the entry-level annual salary for a recording engineer is $18,540. The average salary is $36,970 and the maximum salary is $87,510. According to PayScale.com's Salary Survey Report for Music Recording Engineer, professionals with one to four years of experience are earning an average of $27,772 annually. The figure rises to $45,600 with five to nine years' experience. After 20 years, the average hits $50,000. Payscale.com shows the top three markets as Los Angeles, Chicago, and New York. Average salary for those working at a company was at $48,796 compared to $40,000 for those who are self-employed.

Sound Designer

A sound designer is really the sound director on a project—whether it is a TV show, radio program, or film. More recently, sound designers have found employment working on computer and console games. Play *Halo, Dead Space, World of Warcraft*, or *Grand Theft Auto*, and you will know that the production of the sound, music, and effects is equal or, in some cases, even better than in major motion pictures. Sound design in games has become such an art that the Game Audio Network Guild (http://www.audiogang.org) dedicates itself to championing the work of music and sound effects teams in the game industry. While a sound designer does not usually compose music, he or she may decide on what music is best and how and where it best fits into a film, game, or show. Sound designers work very closely with directors of projects to make sure they are fulfilling the directorial vision. All the sounds put together are sometimes referred to as the soundscape.

When working on a film or show, sound designers study the script carefully so they understand the moods to be created and all the sound effects needed. They may collaborate with a sound effects editor, who gets the actual aural effects needed. They may consult with a composer as well to make sure the music is meshing with each scene. As they develop the final "soundscape," they will gauge the work on some very basic criteria, including pitch (the wavelength of frequency of sound), volume (the loudness), quality (no distortion), and duration. In a theatrical production, the sound designer develops a cue sheet that goes along with the script so recorded sounds and music can be played at the right moments in the play.

These designers shape and direct the overall sounds, dialogue, and music for a film, TV show, play, or video game. It is really a technical and creative field in which the designer uses all audio components and tools to support the final artwork. The title was first conferred on Walter Murch by Francis Ford Coppola for his audio work in the movie *Apocalypse Now*. According to Indeed.com, the average salary for a sound designer is $72,000.

Sound Effects Editor

When you watch a TV show, movie, or video game, or listen to certain radio commercials and programs, you may hear footsteps, gunshots, crashes, strong winds, horses galloping, and other sounds that add to the project. When the sound and story are good—and meshing—you may hardly be aware of the sound. Sound effects editors are the specialists who make sure all the noises—other than the actors' voices—sound just right.

Typically, a sound editor steps in to a project during postproduction. This is the stage of a project when the majority of a project has been filmed and recorded but now the extra touches are added in. They may work with a sound designer on a film, consulting as to what sounds are needed and how they will best mesh in. They often have to build sound effects from scratch using their own imagination: a knife plunged into a watermelon may provide the perfect sound for a horror-movie stabbing or a growling dog slowed down on a tape may be perfect for a monster's roar. Sometimes the person creating these sounds is called a Foley artist and the sound effects editor works with that person. Often, the editor doubles as a Foley artist. Professional effects editors may also develop their own computer library of original sounds, keeping them well-organized and cataloged for easy access on a computer hard drive. MIDI (musical instrument digital interface) programs are well suited for storing sound effects.

The sound effects editor performs the final part of the "postproduction" on a film or TV show, putting together all the sounds, voices, music, and at the proper levels. Employment in the motion picture and video industries is expected to grow 11 percent between 2006 and 2016, according to the Bureau of Labor Statistics (BLS). Opportunities are arising from demand for more content on cable and satellite TV, as well as for programming found on the Internet. Almost all major productions hire union-affiliated workers. The unions guarantee wage levels and provide benefits to members.

Studio Manager

These professionals are similar to house managers in theaters; they make sure the operations of a studio are running smoothly on a daily basis. Managers may handle the booking of studio time, payroll, and employee and intern schedules. Depending on the size of a recording studio, they may answer phones, check inventory of equipment, and make sure the kitchen is stocked with snacks, coffee, tea, and beverages.

Supporting Technical Careers

The following careers are essential supporting occupations and all are related to the recording process. While these positions are important positions in their own right, they often a stepping stone or training ground for a more advanced career to come.

Assistant Engineer

Assistants basically work at the engineer's side, so they can aid in the recording process and learn the ropes. As might be expected, they do more of the "dirty work." Assistants set up microphones, and patch and route cables and cords to the appropriate inputs and outputs. They may have to go on a coffee run for the talent, get snacks, take inventory of equipment, and clean up messes. This is a position for learning and paying dues before moving up the ladder. Usually the lower-level engineers are called "runners" who are running the lower-level tasks. Some larger studios will advance an assistant to a position as second engineer as they master more advanced audio engineering skills and gain experience dealing with equipment and artists.

Mix Engineer

This is a specialty often handled by the recording engineer, and as the name implies this professional focuses solely on the mix of the music. This engineer puts together all the recorded elements to create the final piece. He or she edits and adds such qualities as equalization, effects, and volume balance consistency. The mix engineer keeps up with popular music to bring that aesthetic to the final product, and follows musical direction from the producer and artist. Once the mix is completed, the mix engineer will get a copy to the producer and recording artist to get feedback, and if changes are required, the mix engineer can go back and remix the recording.

Production Assistant

This is the producer's immediate assistant who handles all the essential details for a producer. Although there can be overlap with the studio manager's responsibilities, the assistant schedules sessions, contacts the talent with information, answers e-mails about a project, and makes sure everything is set up and ready to go before a recording session starts. The production assistant gets an up-close look at how producing and engineering works. It is a good position for learning the nuts and bolts of the industry, and from which to advance to producing and assisting with the recording process itself.

Sound Engineering Technician

This title may also be the same as assistant engineer depending on the employer. Technicians like this who assist in recording sound may also work in concert venues, sports arenas, and theaters, and as part of movie or television crews. They set up, operate, and maintain equipment to record, synchronize, mix, and reproduce music, voices, or sound effects. On movie and television production sets, sound techs (also sometimes called production assistants or PAs) may operate the boom microphones or the large overhead mics that are used to record the voices of actors without being seen by the cameras. Their official title may be boom operator in this environment. They may assist in all aspects of recording sound. Those who work assisting in sound recording for film may have the title of *film recordist*. Some technicians take care of maintenance and repair as well, and they need to know about the functions of audio electronics and circuitry. These maintenance technicians employ hands-on tools like wire cutters, screwdrivers, soldering guns, and more to make necessary repairs.

These professionals carry out many of the functions of a recording engineer, although in some recording studios the technicians are the assistants to the engineer. The technician will set up all the equipment and make sure everything is functioning, but the engineer will handle the actual mixing board to record the music. Overall employment of sound engineers is expected to grow through 2016, according to Bureau of Labor Statistics (BLS) research. Median annual earnings of sound engineering technicians were $43,010, according to 2006 data. The middle 50 percent earned between $20,880 and $45,310, while the lowest 10 percent earned less than $21,050 and the highest 10 percent earned more than $90,770. Audio and video equipment technicians are related to this profession and often duties overlap. Also, sound engineering technicians, film recordists, and boom operators are often grouped together as the professionals who assist in capturing the audio properly when filming a movie or television show.

Related Recording Industry Careers

The recording industry also supports professionals who may not be directly involved in the recording process but are key to the industry as a whole. While many of these positions do not invole technical or artistic backgrounds, many employed in the essential supporting roles gain an insider's knowledge of the industry.

Accountant

Most businesses employ accountants and the recording industry is no different. The Web site for Today's CPA (certified public accountants) profiles an accountant whose clients are mostly music store retailers, musicians, independent record labels, and recording studios. He took his love of music and accounting skills and combined them to work with clients and matters that he is passionate about. Accountants generally help ensure that the finances of a business are in order so the firm can operate smoothly. They make sure taxes are paid accordingly and on time. According to the Bureau of Labor Statistics, accountants offer budget analysis, financial and investment planning, information technology consulting, and limited legal services. Most accountants have at least a four-year degree in accounting.

Broadcast Technician and Radio Operator

As the Bureau of Labor Statistic's *Occupational Outlook* states, operator, technician, and engineer are all titles often used interchangeably to describe the same job. As with most work related to the recording industry, computers have taken over. At radio and television stations, computer hard drives and other computer data storage systems are now the main means for storing and accessing audio and video information. Technicians who succeed in this area must master computer networking and software skills. Broadcast technicians have a unique set of skills related to the transmission of signals. They may monitor and log outgoing signals; operate transmitters; and set up, adjust, service, and repair electronic broadcasting equipment. The Bureau of Labor Statistics states that the best training for becoming a technician is to get a degree from a technical school, community college, or a four-year school that offers courses in broadcast technology, electronics, or computer networking.

These professions are closely related to those in the recording industry because they deal with sound equipment used for TV and radio broadcast, concerts, musicals, TV shows, and movies. Employment is expected to grow faster than the average, but growth is predicted to slow with the consolidation of ownership of radio and TV stations and automated equipment. Opportunities are expected from a move toward digital broadcast, which will require installing and operating new digital transmitters. Again, cable television will offer possible employment. Median annual earnings for broadcast technicians in May 2006 were $30,690 according to BLS data. Median annual earnings for radio operators were at $37,890.

Customer Service Representative/ Technical Support

Recording equipment manufacturers also need staff to answer phone calls from customers with questions on equipment. These reps are often well versed in a product and can explain in detail how items operate and how to troubleshoot or install gear, and can guide users step-by-step through specific procedures and functions. Sometimes very detailed questions about equipment are handled by technical support staff who have a more detailed knowledge of product. In general this career requires strong verbal communication skill and possibly some technical background depending on the position, however, no specified college degree is needed.

Studio Designer/Architect

Designers and architects have expertise on how to construct studios that have great acoustics and are well suited to capture sounds. They understand the principles of acoustic design and soundproofing. They unite comfort and appropriate lighting with the recording equipment needed. The career combines knowledge of both audio equipment and architecture. Today's architects use computer-aided design to plan recording studio structures. Although not essential, many studio designers have degrees in architecture. There are 114 schools of architecture that offer degree programs accredited by the National Architectural Accrediting Board, according to the Bureau of Labor Statistics. The most common professional degree in architecture is the five-year bachelor's degree program. Those with an undergraduate degree in architecture can get a two-year master's degree; those with an undergraduate degree in another subject can complete a three- or four-year master's in architecture. All architects must meet state licensing requirements.

Sometimes called an acoustical architect, those who specialize in building facilities that are perfect for recording sound earn a range when it comes to annual wages, but median annual earning of wage-and-salary architects were $64,150, according to latest BLS research.

Recording Industry Talent Careers

The recording industry is nothing without the creative material to record. The following careers are all those that involve the making of the actual music and other types of creative audio content.

Music Composer

Music compositions fuel the recording industry. The works can be purely instrumental or combined with lyrics. Composers are thought of separately from songwriters as they often compose larger pieces of music than just single songs. Composers make music for specific theater works, Broadway musicals, films, and television shows. Composers can work with many genres of music from pop to classical to jazz. They have strong backgrounds in music theory and composition, and they have to know how to play music and how parts played on various instruments will combine to make a fluid piece of music. Typically, composers are educated at music schools or conservatories. Some composers strive to get their works played live by an orchestra to gain recognition. Composing music for an independent film or other low-budget project can often be a proving ground and a way to display talent. To get more information on this field, check the Web site for the National Association of Composers (http://www.music-usa.org/nacusa). Careers related to that of composer are arranger or adapter and copyist. The arranger will take a musical composition and construct it (or reconstruct it) for a specific project, or tailor it for a specific band, orchestra, artist, or ensemble. The original music is intact but the arranger may determine how it can be presented with different voices and instruments. The arranger may also alter the tempo, rhythm, and harmonic structure of a musical composition. A copyist performs the exacting job of transferring musical parts onto staff paper from a score, although the job has become somewhat easier with development of computer software for music copyists.

The talent who writes the music for the recorded music and songs have wide ranging salaries. Many receive broadcast and publishing royalties that boost their earnings. The Bureau of Labor Statistics (BLS) reports that the annual median salary for a composer in 2004 was $34,570. According to PayScale.com, the median annual salary for a composer with 10 to 19 years' experience is $73,986.

Musician

Musician is one of the widest ranging career categories. The term encompasses the accordionist in a polka band to the classical guitarist who plays Sunday brunches to the violinist in a symphony orchestra to the drummer in Metallica. Some musicians accompany dance troupes, while others work in piano bars. Career paths are very divergent for musicians but they all require a passion for music. While any type of musician may be involved in a recording, certain session players specialize in being available for recording sessions. Only the pros thrive and succeed, so session musicians have to be totally skilled at their instrument and be able to read music. The description of "plays well with others" is essential to this career because session musicians have to adapt to all different styles of music to get employment. Many develop their musical "chops" by studying in college and then playing as much as possible.

While some musicians may hold salaried positions with an orchestra or receive a regular check while working in the pit at a Broadway show, many have unsteady work. They take gigs as they come (weddings, bar mitzvahs, nighttime shows), but they have to supplement the performance by working jobs with more regular paychecks. Many teach in addition to performing. Like singers, musicians have to maintain good physical health to play their instrument at their best. This can be especially difficult when touring for several weeks or even months. Many musicians belong to the American Federation of Musicians (http://www.afm.org), which helps ensure they receive fair compensation as well as benefits such as health care and pensions. While musicians can be self-taught, many refine their craft by studying music in a college.

Musicians are essential to the recording industry since they are the talent providing the material for the actual recording. Like producers, their salaries vary wildly from millions of dollars to about $7 an hour, according to the BLS. Recent BLS data shows that median hourly wages for musicians were about $19.73. Musicians typically do not have regular employment. About 35 percent of musicians work part-time; 48 percent were self-employed. Most opportunities are in major cities such as New York, Los Angeles, Nashville, and Chicago. Employment is expected to grow about as fast as the average for all positions, according to the BLS, and most new staff positions (as opposed to freelance) are anticipated in religious organizations. BLS projects 11 percent growth for musicians overall, but only 5 percent for those who work in nightclubs, concert halls, and other venues. Talented studio musicians may find more steady income than other musicians as they are often sought after for recording sessions. Musicians who have a hit song will also earn more from sales, broadcast fees, and licensing songs to TV and movies.

Music Supervisor

When you hear popular songs in a film or television show, they may have been selected by a music supervisor (also called a music coordinator or music director). The music supervisor for the television show *The OC*, for example, has been responsible for getting cutting-edge music from Belle & Sebastian, Band of Horses, Lady Sovereign, and other musical acts. A music supervisor may decide what songs best enhance a project, and then he or she will negotiate usage licenses and handle legal contract negotiations, typically dealing with budget concerns and process all necessary paperwork. Those wanting to enter the field may work on independent films to secure rights to songs. Demonstrating appropriate musical taste for a project and the ability to obtain song rights on a budget can be the springboard into a fulltime career as a supervisor. Music supervisors may come from a performing musician background, but there is not a set advanced educational requirement for entering this field.

Singer

While most songwriters are also singers, not all singers are songwriters. While many singers strive to be "stars," they often take advantage of the many opportunities that are not in the spotlight: jobs as background vocalists, opera singers, choir singers, Broadway musical cast singers, and more. As with many performance careers, singers typically start by performing wherever and whenever they can, often for very little, if any, money. Those who become established popular singers have to spend long stretches of time on the road touring to promote their music and recordings. They also block out time to record, and they certainly know their way around a recording studio. Most singers are driven by the thrill of performing and receiving the applause and attention. Earning money at this career can be challenging as there are few high-paying positions for singers. Talented singers can find employment working as vocal teachers.

While some singers will train in music and voice, others have a natural talent. Some singers are not traditionally good, but they have attitude, charisma, and style that attracts an audience. Opera singers and stage singers typically have years of studying voice. Many study singing in college or with independent voice teachers who teach them how to maintain pitch, breathe, stay on key, and other essentials. Even when singers write their own material, they have to be on the lookout for good songs (and songwriters) so they can keep the hits coming. Like songwriters (discussed below), singers have to maintain their body and stay in shape. Their body and voice is their instrument and if they are over-exhausted, out of shape, or not eating right, their vocal delivery can suffer.

Songwriter

Irving Berlin. John Lennon and Paul McCartney. Carole King. Jay-Z. They are each famous songwriters who have made millions of dollars by writing popular songs. Naturally, most songwriters do not earn these sums but the potential is there, especially if the writer can come up with an enduring hit. Those who enter this career have a deep musical creative streak and almost a compulsion to write songs, combining words and music. The career requires much perseverance and almost luck to create a song that captures the public's imagination and becomes the "hot" song of the moment.

Songwriters have to be incredibly talented. Most start out as singers, either performing as a solo act or with a band. To advance their careers, songwriters may try to get an agent and get signed to a record label. Successful songwriters make deals with publishers who try to place their songs in movies, television shows, and other media that will generate royalties and profits for both the writer and the publisher. Publishers may claim a large percentage of royalties but, in exchange, they may give the writer a sizable advance on the future earnings of a song. Top songwriters may be able to strike a deal whereby they earn a salary from the publisher. Songwriters need as much exposure as possible, so many play live as often as possible. Today's songwriters have to know how to promote their music on the Web as well. Using networking sites like Facebook and MySpace can help. Performing can be exhausting so songwriters have to take good care of themselves. If they get run down, they run the risk of ruining their voice or simply not performing up to par.

A sub-career to songwriter is lyricist, who simply writes the words to music. There have been many hit songs where one party writes the music and the other writes the words. Often, the career is associated with musicals. Oscar Hammerstein wrote the lyrics to *The Sound of Music, Showboat*, and *South Pacific*, and Fred Ebb wrote the lyrics to *Chicago* and *Cabaret*, but neither wrote the music. Lyricist is a narrower field than songwriter, and those who succeed in musical theater have dedication and passion for the art form.

Voice Talent

Some recording studios specialize in recording audio for radio and television commercials, and they rely on actors who have especially strong and compelling voices to deliver commercial messages. For many actors, voiceover work is attractive because they do not have to put on makeup and rehearse lines. They can arrive to a recording studio in sweatpants and read their lines as long as they deliver the words effectively. Many voice actors do other acting jobs, and they may belong to the Screen Actors Guild of SAG (http://www.sag.org) or the American Federation of Television and Radio Artists (http://www.aftra.org). There are many voice acting coaches in the United States and they help budding talent to make demo tapes, which can be crucial to securing a job in this field. For more information on this career, check out the Voice Over International Creative Experience (http://voice-international.com).

Talent Support Careers

These careers are another grouping of supportive occupations that are not directly involved with creating or recording audio content, but they are essential in supporting the creative talent that produces the songs and other types of audio.

Advertising Account Executive

At a record label, the advertising staff creates advertising campaigns for the acts and products. They will decide the best media in which to purchase ad time or space—whether it is in newspapers, magazines, billboards, on subways, online, on the radio, or on TV. This is a very creative field that needs strong communication skills and an understanding of consumer behavior and markets that are most likely to reach the music-buying public. For example, a major label may buy airtime during a popular TV show, such as *Gossip Girl*, that reaches a young music-savvy audience. Professionals who have advertising experience in another field may find it easy to transfer into advertising for a record label.

Artist Relations Representative

This professional performs as almost a diplomat between the label and the artist. He or she conveys the label's concerns and business to the artist, and in turn, the AR rep tells the artist's concerns to the label. Ultimately, the goal is to keep both parties happy, so the job requires strong skills in communication and negotiation. They serve as mediators when problems arise. They may arrange promotional appearances, similar to the role of the publicist, and they may also advise the artists on creative approaches and business matters.

A&R Administrator

Major labels have what are called artist and repertoire departments, and the administrators who work there take care of most clerical duties, many related to tracking cash flow. They estimate artist budgets and track artist expenses. When a recording session is planned, they monitor the costs of studio time, session musicians, producer fees, meals, and other expenses.

A&R Coordinator

These coordinators are talent scouts, always on the lookout for new hot talent that labels can sign. A&R scouts listen to demos, with an ear for what will be the next big thing. When the scout finds a sound he or she likes, the scout alerts the A&R manager who often has the authority to sign an act to a record label. Without A&R coordinators, some acts would have never gotten discovered. A&R people with a proven track record can move up the career ladder. A&R man Gary Gersh brough Nirvana to Geffen Records, a move that established his career and led to his eventually becoming the head of Capitol Records.

Business Manager

In *The Musician's Handbook*, Bobby Borg emphasizes that a business manager is not a personal manager. He states that an artist should consider their personal manager as the chief executive officer of an artist's enterprise while a business manager is more like the CFO (chief financial officer) who manages the income from deals once they are in place. They can establish investment strategies and handle bookkeeping, such as invoices, monthly bills, collecting money owed, and depositing money. A recording studio may have a business manager other than the studio manager but often that's one and the same job. Business managers may also be accountants because those skills of handling financial paperwork are essential to the job. Those who manage the careers of musicians earn an average of $46,000 per year, according to Simplyhired.com.

Concert Promoter

When U2, Aerosmith, Dave Matthews, or the Foo Fighters put on a large concert, they rely on someone to be in charge of organizing the event. The same type of person is needed to stage huge outdoor music festival such as Milwaukee's Summerfest, Coachella in California, and Bonnaroo in Nashville, Tennessee. Promoters enjoy high-energy, high-stress days as they get together music acts, coordinate advertising, raise money to stage the event, and handle the budgeting and finances. The promoter often takes on the financial risk of putting on a concert, but he or she can also reap a large financial reward if the concert is successful.

Entertainment Lawyer

These attorneys specialize in matters related to entertainment. They review and draft contracts for musicians and other entertainers, whether they be about manager relations or terms with a record label. A recording studio may use an entertainment lawyer to write a contract if it is producing a product and getting paid in a percentage of the profits. Some entertainment lawyers have strong industry contacts and they may be able to shop talent or an album to a record label. To get into this career, you must obtain a law degree and specialize in entertainment law.

Music Publisher

Ed Pierson, vice president of business and legal affairs at Warner/Chapell Music calls music publishing "the business of songs." Publishers acquire the copyrights to songs and publish them. Music publishers help place an artist's song in films, TV shows, commercials, Web sites, and computer games, to name a few media outlets. The publishing firm provides the license for a firm to use the material. That company will then pay for the license, and if the material is broadcast, there may be royalties paid to artists and the music publisher. Artists have to understand that when a song earns money from royalties, some of the money goes to the artist who wrote the song, and some goes to the publisher (which can be the artist or a publishing company or a combination).

There are many rights that can be sold in music publishing. Those interested in the field should do further research on mechanical royalties, performance royalties, synchronization fees, print royalties, electronic transmissions, and foreign subpublishing incomes. Mechanical royalties, however, are perhaps the hugest source of income for music publishers. These are licensing fees paid for the use of a song by a record company, film production company, or other outlet. Publishers take some ownership of a song and a percentage of future earnings. In return, the publisher plugs the material to get it placed on TV shows, films, or games. When the song is broadcast, there are royalties

Music publishers help get music performed by popular artists or used in movies, TV shows, and computer games. They earn money by obtaining ownership of some or all of an artist's copyrights or publishing rights, and then they collect the royalties. They focus on getting an artist broadcast as much as possible because the more exposure they get for an artist, the more money they make. Music publishers earn an average annual salary of $42,000, according to Simplyhired.com.

Music Video Director

Music videos have seen their peak in the 1980s and 1990s when MTV was dedicated to showing music videos. However, all top musical acts still have videos to promote their music. Many spread the word by being shown on YouTube and other online sites. Music videos are mini movies that correspond to a song. These directors are just like any regular film directors who have to know all the basics about filming, editing, sound, lighting, costumes, working with actors, and all the other elements that go into making a film. They may hold auditions, create storyboards, and spend hours rehearsing their actors to get each scene just right.

Many of today's famous film directors started out as music video directors, such as Spike Jonze and Michel Gondry. Some music directors have developed long careers specializing in music videos, such as Sophie Muller who has directed music videos for Björk, Hole, Weezer, No Doubt, Beyoncé, and Kings of Leon.

Product Developer

Some record labels, both independents and majors, have a department of product development that focuses on ways to generate sales for new recording. Product developers often serve as marketers and promoters, figuring out a plan to gain attention for a product. But they are also professionals who may make decisions about the recording, packaging, and manufacturing of music. Those in product development may also be involved in artist development as well, developing and maintaining an act's image. Those in artist development may also secure affiliation with performance rights association such as ASCAP, BMI, and SESAC.

Publicist

In general, publicists work for record labels and are in charge of publicity and public relations for an act. An act may hire its own publicist as well. Sometimes called a press agent, the publicist makes sure press releases are sent out to all the media—magazines, newspapers, TV, radio, Internet sites, etc., all with the goal of getting exposure for the client. The trick is convincing the media that the client is news. The publicist may write the press releases as well. They arrange interviews and handle all the scheduling details. They may conceive of special press events and arrange press parties. They have to be "schmoozers" who know how to talk to people.

Radio Disc Jockey

Radio disc jockey is definitely a career that has morphed in the last 20 years. While traditional radio has been on the decline, opportunities have grown in Internet radio and satellite radio. In its *Global Entertainment* and *Media Outlook 2009–2013*, PricewaterhouseCooper forecasts a continual decline in "terrestrial" radio advertising through the year 2013.

Radio, whether traditional terrestrial stations, online, or satellite, is still a primary way that people find and discover recorded music, and it is vital for promoting music. Disc jockeys are the ones playing the music and talking before and after playing songs. The job requires good vocal delivery—generally they have to convey warmth and friendliness over the airwaves. Music knowledge and a quick wit are usually valued in this business. Many start out by proving themselves in college radio or volunteering at community or commercial radio stations. It is worth mentioning that some deejays "spin" music only at dance clubs. The best of these deejays are celebrities in their own right and highly sought after. Popular club disc jockeys can also make a difference in making a song a hit by giving it extensive play.

According the Bureau of Labor Statistics, median hourly earnings of wage and salary radio and television announcers in May 2006 were $11.69. The middle 50 percent earned between $8.10 and $18.62. The lowest 10 percent earned less than $6.55, and the highest 10 percent earned more than $32.98. Median hourly earnings of announcers in the radio and television broadcasting industry were $11.52.

Radio Music Director

Directors are usually the gatekeepers, deciding what music gets played on the air. That's why major labels and independents hire staff to promote their albums to the music directors. Program director is a title closely associated with this career. Sometimes a music director assists the program director in deciding what music should get played; other times they are the same job. A program director often oversees the scheduling and programming of all the broadcasts. The music director also maintains the station's music library.

INTERVIEW

Life Inside a State-of-the-Art Studio

Matt Bien and Paul Goldberg
Owners, Pure Audio, a professional commercial recording
studio in Seattle, Washington

How does Pure Audio as a studio represent the current state of the recording industry?

Bien: Our studio has recorded thousands of radio commercials and is representative of how this segment of the industry works. The studio works with national companies such as Microsoft, Nike, Wells Fargo, ESPN, and T-Mobile, as well as regional companies such a CarToys. Working with big companies has also meant recording big-name talent such as Fergie of the Black-Eyed Peas, the actor Alec Baldwin, cartoonist Gary Larson, and the legendary musician Taj Mahal.

How have you been able to get such high-profile projects?

Goldberg: The studios at Pure Audio are acoustically designed to best capture the sound of the human voice. Working with prestigious clientele means that we have to be very polished and professional. While the company prides itself on top-notch engineering and mixing, it also boasts a very client-friendly atmosphere with comfortable modern furniture and lighting, excellent food for the clients, and an engaging and knowledgeable staff.

Bien: Attention to these details really matters. For example, you want a reputation of always starting a session on time.

What are your facilities like?

Goldberg: Most commercial studios, like Pure Audio, offer an isolation booth, which is usually a very small room with very good soundproofing to keep out all external sounds. The room could be used to capture a voiceover or a single instrument. A studio usually has a big "live" room as well that a whole band can fit into and play at once and is acoustically ideal for recording the live sound.

The latest technology means being able to offer clients a land patch or ISDN (Integrated Services Digital Network), which provides fast and accurate data transmission via a special connection over the phone lines. The system allows a studio to record the voice of a talent anywhere in the country from its home base. For instance, Pure Audio was hired to record Alec Baldwin for a local car commercial, but the actor was vacationing in Cape Cod. He could, however, take off a couple hours to go to a Cape Cod studio and have Pure Audio in Seattle record his voice via an ISDN line. The equipment allows for near-perfect recording of a voice, and listeners are none the wiser that the voice talent may be on opposite coasts from the actual recording studio. And if the client wants to do an in-person recording, the studio has portable gear and can bring a mini-studio to the client.

Pure Audio, like many other mid-sized commercial studios, offers quality phone-in recording equipment for those who cannot get to an ISDN-equipped studio. This type of set-up can be used when an executive at a major corporation wants to record a message and have it delivered to large number of people on his or her staff. The studio records the message via phone and then coordinates that the audio file arrives in each designated employee's e-mail box.

We've talked to many different recording engineers in writing this book and one thing that keeps coming up is the backing up of data. It sounds like studios really have to have a good system for tracking and storing data to succeed in the industry. How do you deal with all the data?

Bien: To be a successful audio engineer today, you have to be excellent at data management. Most multitracked projects create tons of data, such as bass tracks, vocal tracks, guitar tracks, etc. The engineer has to carefully label all these bits of data and be able to retrieve them. While keeping track of this data is an essential part of running a recording studio, engineers also cannot store everything on studio hard drives. They often have to clear the hard drives for new projects. They will commonly provide the artists tracks to a project on a portable FireWire drive. Plus, the artist should also take an additional back up of the data just in case something happens to his or her one and only copy. That is why studios will offer a backup of material often onto digital tapes called AIT tapes.

To succeed in the industry today, or at any time in the past or future, pleasing the client seems to be essential. What are some more of the services you offer that makes you or any studio successful in the industry today?

Goldberg: Sometimes, the ad agency or firm hiring the studio does not already have the talent lined up to do the project, so they turn to the studio to audition voice talent and make a final selection. The studio may also add in music from its library or hire musicians to come in and play specific music for an advertisement. If the client suddenly wants three trombones on the project, we'll find them three trombones.

(continues on next page)

INTERVIEW

Life Inside a State-of-the-Art Studio (continued)

Trafficking is another essential part of being a successful commercial studio. Pure Audio may record a T-Mobile spot to be broadcast at 400 radio stations. Each spot might be a little different, but the correct audio file must be delivered on time to the appropriate person at each station with all the correct information attached. Being able to handle this type of distribution on a large-scale basis is essential for making it in the commercial recording industry.

Are there other business basics that anyone working in a recording studio should know about?
Bien: Proper handling of all the business aspects is essential for a studio to survive and to thrive. The studio needs an efficient, fair, and accurate billing system to assure income is coming in and that clients are receiving timely invoices. Clients respect the attention to detail and professionalism and keep coming back, and word spreads about the quality of an operation. A studio like Pure Audio must also promote itself to ad agencies, corporations, and other entities to make sure people know about its services. A commercial recording studio like us distributes brochures detailing the types of equipment it uses, and the numbers of studios it offers, as well as listing former clients and types of projects. A studio also has to maintain its own Web page, and many keep a presence on MySpace.

Radio Promoter

All promoters are about generating buzz for their clients or events. Radio promoters naturally try to get airplay for the acts they represent. The job requires strong people skills as promoters call up music directors, program directors, and disc jockeys at radio stations and sing the praises of their clients and encourage them to play the music. Independent artists often hire independent radio promoters to try and get their music more exposure. They send radio stations artist CDs and background information and then spend time calling the music programmers to convince them to play the music. A version of this career is *college promoter*. Some labels have promotions

Goldberg: To succeed in the recording industry today you have to focus on core competency and elevate your game to the highest level possible. You don't just focus on recording as an art. You have to focus on the business aspects as well. You have to interface with corporations on a very professional level. Our customers take for granted that we're very good at what we do. What separates us is our ability to be creative but fulfill the business aspects. We provide the stability so clients are confident that their project is going to be completed on time and successfully.

What technology do you specialize in that gives you a cutting-edge and reflects the state of the industry today?
Bien: We record audio for television shows and films and use a process called Audio Digital Replacement (ADR), or looping. This method is used in creating many films and television shows to make sure the audio is the best it can be. When ADR is used in a movie, often all the actors have to come into the recording studio and re-record every bit of dialogue that was shot in the film. Trying to get the sound perfect when filming can be difficult and expensive, so the studios and producers making a film ultimately find it more cost-effective to re-record voices in the studio and give them the proper mix in the film. Even though located in Seattle, far from the bulk of the film and TV industry in New York City and Hollywood, our expertise in ADR work has landed us major projects, such as handling the audio on Stephen King's *Rose Red* TV mini-series. You have to diversify as well. As a recording studio, we cannot survive by just doing commercial or film work. In recent years, we have been doing more and more audio for electronic games.

people who are dedicated to hyping their clients only on campuses. They are often dealing with the college radio stations and student affairs.

Record Store Owners

Record shop owners earned an average of $46,000 a year, according to SimplyHired.com. Although more and more sales are via the Internet and many large chains have closed, there are at least 1,000 independent record stores in the United States, according to the Coalition of Independent Record Stores.

Sales Representative

With CD sales dropping in recent years, it may seem a tough path to pursue a career in retail sales. The market research firm the Almighty Institute of Music Retail (http://www.almightyretail.com) reports that more than 1,300 independent record stores have closed in the United States since 2003. However, the Institute says that at least 1,000 independent stores exist around the country and many have banded together to promote events like Record Store Day. Many independents thrive by catering to loyal independent music fans. With major chains like the Virgin Megastores and Tower Records now gone, a music fan can still get work in a CD shop and learn about all the latest music, but the outlook for a long-term career is uncertain in CD and record sales. On the label side, there are also salespeople who service the retail stores and provide them with product.

Salespeople are still in demand to sell musical gear and instruments at stores such at Guitar Center and audio equipment at large chains like Best Buy. Recording equipment manufacturers have their own sales reps who are in contact with studios and handle the sales of recording gear. They may also work at trade shows where they explain and demonstrate the latest equipment.

Talent Manager

This professional is also called a music manger, artist manager, or booking agent and handles many of the business aspects of an artist's career so the talent can focus on being creative. While talent agents can work independently many work for talent agencies and represent more than one artist. Two of the biggest and most famous talent agencies in the country are the William Morris Agency and Creative Artists Agency. If you have seen the hit cable TV show *Entourage*, the character Ari (portrayed by Jeremy Piven) is a talent agent. Talent agents aggressively work to get their client work and sometimes publicity (although that work can fall to the publicist). They negotiate contracts for performances and take care of billing and collecting payments. They may also possibly arrange recording deals for the artist they represent. Depending on the manager, they may handle many of the artist's personal affairs as well, telling them what events to show up at and planning social engagements. Sometimes roles will be divided up and an artist may have a personal manager and a separate booking agent. According to Bobby Borg in *The Musician's Handbook*, managers usually work for a commission and the commission is usually substantial (between 15 and 30 percent of an artist's earnings) because they invest time, reputation, and money with no guarantee of payoff.

Artists sign contracts specifying the terms of their relationship with a manager, including details about exclusivity, manager responsibilities, and payment. In general, artists and managers want a personal connection so they can get along and further each other's careers. However, the music industry has many stories of manager-artists relationships that have gone sour. Trent Reznor, the front man of Nine Inch Nails, for example, charged his manager with cheating him out of millions of dollars by doing things that Reznor said went against their contract. The case went to court and the jury awarded Reznor $2.95 million with interest, bringing the total to $4 million.

The *Musician's Handbook* makes a distinction between personal manager and talent agent, although there can be overlap. The personal manager advises and counsels the artist, but the talent agent actually gets the musician work. No matter what the role played by an agent, pay is usually based on some type of commission.

Tour Coordinator

When a band gets ready to hit the road, they rely on a tour coordinator to take care of all the details. The coordinator figures out all the travel plans, means of transportation, food, and lodging. They may make sure that the band is running on schedule, making it to sound checks on time, and keeping up with media appearances along the way. They keep careful track of all expenses and try to keep their acts on budget so they do not spend more than they are earning in ticket sales.

Visual/Graphic Artist

Although not involved with the audio aspects of the recording industry, graphic artists play an important role in the success of a label or artist. Graphic artists come up with packing for CDs, posters, stickers, T-shirts, and advertisements. They may dream up a band's distinctive logo—think of the type treatment for a band like Led Zeppelin or when Prince had a distinctive symbol that represented his name.

Successful graphic artists in the recording business have a keen sense of marketing—they create with a mind for what will sell. For those who artistically inclined and love the music and recording biz, this is a great way to be a part of it. Getting a foot in the door requires a portfolio showcasing a range of styles and samples of music-related designs that could be used for CD jackets or other merchandise. Many get training at a school of visual arts or a college graphic design program. While they are adept at drawing, painting, and other standard art skills, they also need to know about computer design and type treatments.

Those who design the CD jackets, posters, T-shirts, and marketing materials are essential to the success of the recording industry. Median annual earnings for wage and salary graphic designers were $39,900 in May 2006. The middle 50 percent earned between $30,600 and $53,310. The lowest 10 percent earned less than $24,120, and the highest 10 percent earned more than $69,730.

Chapter 4

Tips for Success

While the only real course for succeeding in the music and recording business is real-life experience, there are certain tips that can help you thrive and further your professional goals as you find your direction in the industry.

Even Giants Started Small

Some of the biggest names in the industry started out in humble posts. David Geffen founded the Geffen record label, which put out hit albums by Bob Dylan and Peter Gabriel, among others. Partnering with Steven Spielberg and Jeffrey Katzenberg, he went on to form the entertainment enterprise known as DreamWorks SKG. Geffen started his career in entertainment from the lowly spot of the mailroom at the William Morris talent agency. From this position, he became a talent agent trainee and saw firsthand the ins and outs of the entertainment business. Simon Cowell, who created *American Idol* and has served as its most curmudgeonly talent judge, started his career as a mailroom clerk for EMI Music Publishing. He worked his way up in the industry until he became a record producer.

Like Geffen and Cowell, if you are passionate about getting ahead in the recording industry, prepare to do some of the grunt work first. If you have zero experience, you may take any type of low-level job in a studio. Do not discount the job of cleaner, the person who scrubs the kitchen counters, cleans the toilets, washes the dishes, and takes out the trash. The Web site Recordproduction.com claims that many people who now operate major studios started out as the cleaner at a studio. Receptionist is another position that you should not write off. The person who answers the phones and meets and greets clients is in a perfect spot for making valuable networking connections. The lowest-level technician spot is the runner (also known as the gofer), and it is well labeled since this job involves a lot of running—to the post office, to the Chinese restaurant for food, or to make deliveries across town.

From any low-rung position, you can learn who is who in the company and a bit about what they do. You can get a sense of how a business operates. By developing connections with other employees, you can ask questions about different positions and what it takes to succeed in those jobs. Often, if a studio is shorthanded for a particular task they will turn to the new workers to lend a hand. This is a great opportunity to learn. No one wants to get stuck in a grunt-work job. This is a stepping-stone, and while you will be expected to do your time carrying out menial tasks, keep moving toward a higher goal.

Once you get a sense of the type of activities you would like to be involved with, you can ask to assist in your off hours on the projects that most interest you.

Internships are especially good for learning job skills, and while you may have already been working a few years, those who have specific career goals in mind may still consider taking an internship even after having worked in the industry. Many internships do not pay, or pay very little, but provide real-life experienc and the opportunity to make professional connections for those trying to change direction or expand into a new area. Again, interns wind up doing the menial tasks at first. But if they are around and show a willingness to pitch in, superiors will turn to them and get them involved in meaningful projects. To make the most of an internship, you should set some personal and professional goals for yourself. By doing this, you will be striving for exactly what you want in your career. Try to schedule meetings with your supervisor to discuss your goals, projects, and possible future opportunities. If your boss does not give you one, you might even ask for a performance review so you can evaluate your strengths and contributions, and where you need room for improvement. Always try to keep a positive outlook—positive energy can go a long way, and negative energy will block opportunities for you.

Finding a Mentor

The word *mentor* goes back to Greek mythology, where Athena, the goddess of wisdom, transformed into the form of Mentor to give advice to Odysseus. If you have been in the recording industry a few years, you may identify potential mentors in your place of employment. You may try to network with someone you admire professionally, perhaps inviting that person out to lunch to ask him or her questions about their position.

The Web site for the National Association of Recording Industry Professionals (NARIP) says that professional organizations like theirs may be a more effective route to finding a mentor. NARIP has its own Mentor Program. Potential clients are asked to fill out a questionnaire, which allows them to be matched with industry volunteers, according to mutual goals and needs. Once you find a potential mentor match, keep these tips in mind:

→ **Schedule Regular Meetings.** Many begin mentorships with good intentions. They have an initial lunch and a few phone calls but then they get busy and the mentor relationship falls apart. However, if you schedule a regular meeting every four to six weeks, then it becomes a routine that can help you gain significant advice and direction.

→ **Come Prepared.** Before you meet, know what you want to talk about. You might want to bring up some of your goals and ask for pointers on how you might reach them. You might ask your mentor for suggestions of books, conferences, workshops, professional organizations, and other resources that can give you a leg up in the industry.

→ **Don't Be a Pest.** Try to stick to your regular appointments with a mentor and do not be afraid to call occasionally with a specific question. But do not be too pushy or constantly in contact. Make sure your mentor has breathing room, and if they get busy, it is OK to skip the regular meeting now and then.

→ **Show Respect.** Always remember that the mentor is giving his or her time to you. Make sure you are always on time to meetings. Be polite. Be attentive to all he or she says.

➤ **Evaluate If Your Mentorship Is Working.** After a few mentor meetings, take a step back and ask yourself if you are truly getting helpful advice, job leads, and information that is furthering your goals. If the mentorship is not working for you, you will have to be honest, end your relationship, and start looking for another. Like any relationship, a good mentor relationship can be a matter of chemistry and that can take some time to develop.

Become a Networker

All activities where you can talk to or socialize with coworkers, bosses, or colleagues in the industry can help you find out about opportunities that will advance your career. If a coworker invites you out to socialize with other coworkers, jump at the chance. If there is a company volleyball or softball team, sign up. You can always take the initiative as well and invite a colleague to lunch and informally inquire about what he or she does and ask about possible opportunities that person may know about.

To meet more people in your field, you may want to call up professional recording industry associations and see if you can join. By attending trade shows and seminars, sponsored by groups such as the National Association of Recording Industry Professionals (NARIP), you will not only have the chance to meet others in your field, you will learn about the latest trends, technology, and job developments. At industry events, you can find out who are the movers and shakers in the business and make contacts with potential employers. Ask professional groups about volunteer opportunities—not only a great way to network, but a great way to master more skills as well. You might look into joining groups online as well where you can post questions and meet others who are starting out in the business. The Just Plain Folks music organization (http://www.jpfolks.com) offers forums where you can post anything music related and possibly find a mentor. The site boasts having 18,000+ mentors in just about every type of music profession, including gold and platinum songwriters, managers, legal professionals, recording artists, publishers, and manufacturers.

It is best to define your own goals before you begin seriously networking. Those who can help with your career will ask about your interests and what you would like to achieve. So carefully think about where you are heading and where you would like to be a few years into your career. When you do make a golden contact—someone who may have a job lead or a real position to offer, do the right thing. Make sure you have that person's contact information. Soon after meeting you should follow up with an e-mail expressing your interest and highlighting your talents. You never know when opportunity will come knocking, so it is important to keep your résumé up-to-date and ready to send.

An Informational Interview

When you meet someone in the business who can share valuable information about a career with you, you may want to set up what's called an informational interview These are casual meetings at lunch or over the phone. They should be fun, interesting, and low pressure. On the surface, it is just two people getting together for some ordinary conversation, but if you are hunting for opportunities, you really need to prepare. Think what questions you would like to ask on an informational interview: How did you get started? What was your educational and employment background? What do you enjoy most about your work? What are your responsibilities? What's a typical workweek like? What skills do you need to get into this business? What advice overall would you give a person like me who is looking to land a position?

Diverse Skills Pay Off

At a seminar offered by the National Association of Recording Industry Professionals (NARIP) titled "Strategies for Survival & Success in a Shrinking Record Industry Job Market in Los Angeles," industry professionals admitted that currently many opportunities have been shrinking. However those with diverse skills are most employable. For example, the recording engineer who has experience mixing sound for film, recording bands in the studio, and handling the live sound at a concert has the diversity that is more likely to land a position. The people who are most sought after are those who have skills transferable to other parts of the entertainment business, such as movies, television, and consumer products, panelist Jeremy Eskenazi, director of strategic staffing for the Universal Music Group and Universal Corporate, told attendees. The panel discussed how opportunities are there for those who understand rapidly evolving technologies like music applications for cell phone and handheld devices. Hot tips from this seminar included: Taking control over your career and mapping a course for yourself. Taking risks like

Everyone
Knows

Work Traits That Lead to Success

These tips apply to any job and you should follow them if you want to get ahead. You may already know these basics, but it is good to review them once in awhile to make sure you are on track with some of these business fundamentals.

- **Always be on time.** Every employer values punctuality and many will not tolerate lateness. Be late a few times in a row and you may find yourself out of a job. By the same token, do not leave at 4:59 if the day ends at 5 pm. Put in extra time until the work gets done. And do not take an extra long lunch.

- **Be eager to learn.** Employers value those who want to find out more about operations and chip in where needed.

- **Know you are being evaluated.** When you start a job, employers often consider the first few weeks a "probationary period." They will be keeping a close eye on you, your attitude, and performance. You should know the exact terms of this evaluation period.

- **Keep a neat desk.** A messy desk does not make a good impression. Do not go postering up your favorite rock bands, keeping soda cans on your desktop, and storing stinky gym shorts and shoes in your work area.

- **Get all your basic tools right away.** Find out if you need an office key or lock codes. You may need passwords for computers and codes for a copy machine as well. Make sure you have the

moving to another country. Reading everything. Starting your own business. Not being a nine-to-fiver; doing whatever it takes to get the job done. Getting involved in community service and becoming your company's rep.

Develop Clients and Experience

Compared to other fields, the recording industry is very competitive, and success depends more on who you know than in other fields. When it comes to getting an engineering job with a major studio, the basic office supplies you need for your job: paper, stapler, fold-ers—whatever you require. You may need special equipment as well, depending on your position. Some companies will require that you log your hours and keep careful track.

- **Know the rules and protocol.** Every business has its distinct rules of operation. Be sure you go over them with your boss or someone who works in human resources.

- **Take the initiative.** If you find yourself with nothing to do, ask your superior how you can help. Do not use downtime to goof off—answering personal e-mails, surfing the Web, etc.

- **Take responsibility for mistakes.** We all goof up sometimes. When you do make a mistake, tell what the mistake is and sug-gest ways that it can be corrected.

- **Be ready for a performance review.** Most businesses give their employees a review at least once a year. Raises, bonuses, promo-tions, and simply continuing your employment depend on how you do in a review, so when yours comes up, be ready. Make a list of your accomplishments and how you have been contributing to the company. Take criticism well. Listen and ask for suggestions on how to improve or make your own suggestions. Take notes so you know what you should be doing to improve and what your boss expects in the months ahead.

- **Maintain workplace etiquette.** Do not be a gossip. Do not date someone you work with.

studio may want to know that you have connections with musicians and other industry professionals. This is a job where it really pays to be outgoing.

Before Scott Hull became the owner of Masterdisk, he worked as an employee there, observing how business was conducted. Some engineers at Masterdisk would hang out with bands, go out at night, and always be "social butterflies." He saw these engineers as party animals and did not think they'd last long in the business. But the "party animal" engineers would continue to get clients and get work. "They may not have been the best engineers," says Hull, "but they were really good salesmen." When it got slow at Masterdisk, these "social" engineers went out and made themselves known to people. Hull points out that colleges that teach recording engineering focus on the audio and technology, but they rarely spend time on how to present services in a way that is salable.

Hull points out that even while you are socializing, you can be selling yourself and your services. It is a subtle balance between being friendly and selling, and it is something that those entering the business perfect over time. "You have to know how to sell yourself," he says. "A year before I put my own shingle out and opened Scott Hull Mastering in 2005, I realized that mastering engineers were salesmen. It took me a long time to make that connection. Ultimately, the lawyer and the doctor and architect are all salesmen. They need to be to build their business. It was a grand awakening for me, so I got better at selling."

Hull recommends that every beginning recording engineer take a sales and marketing course or two. Hull can easily train people with audio engineering skills, but he wants to hire those who can self-promote, sell their services, and bring people in the door. Some applicants come to Hull with full education on how to master and engineer, but they do not have any potential clients. "Sorry. But I have to hire people who have put up their own shingle. They've been working independently, and now they want to work at a full-fledged studio. I hire those who believe they can bring X number of projects into the studio in the weeks or months ahead."

Hull warns that the worst approach is to come into an interview and say that you want to work at his studio so you can learn as much as possible, meet as many clients as possible, and then eventually open your own studio. You cannot land a job at Masterdisk if you are pitching yourself as someone who will eventually steal clients away.

Those starting in the engineering field may build clients by having a home studio and recording artists for free or a low-rate at first. This helps build a professional relationship with musicians who then may want to go on and work in a pro studio at some point. They may also work in clubs doing live sound and meeting new bands on a nightly basis. Impressing a band with how you mix their live sound can lead to studio work. (You can read anecdotes about mixing live sound and find out about the latest technology at Live Sound International: http://www.livesoundint.com.)

Take Opportunities As They Come

Gil Shuster is now the technical director at the Greene Performance Space at WNYC Radio in New York City. Gil engineers the sound in the room, which was created for live performances, signature WNYC radio shows, and video Webcasts. To get to this position, Gil first worked learning sound as an engineer in a small independent studio in Brooklyn. He also worked as an engineer at WFMU, a popular independent music station based in Jersey City, New Jersey, and as live music engineer at several small clubs in New York City. While these early jobs may not have been high paying, they gave him the experience and background needed to learn his current position as technical director.

Emery Dobyns worked for free as an intern at Dubway Studios in New York City and in the process learned about electrical and audio engineering. Dobyns did not study engineering at college, but mastered the skills in the workplace. He also a worked a variety of different jobs before finding his path as an engineer. Although he was working for free at Dubway Studios, he proved himself on the job. An engineer familiar with his work recommended Dobyns for an assistant engineer's position at Diddy's studio. After a two-week trial, he was hired and began engineering on some major projects, including Nelly's 2003 hit single "Shake Ya Tail Feather." From there, he went on to producing, mixing, and recording work with the artists Antony and the Johnsons, Travis, and at Bad Boy Records. He toured with Patti Smith, mixing her live sound at shows in 2007 in support of her album of covers titled *Twelve*. In 2008, he won a Grammy for engineering Suzanne Vega's album *Beauty and Crime*.

Develop an "Audio Portfolio"

Many of the positions in the recording industry require that you show an "audio portfolio." This would be a sampling of the best of your recorded work if you are seeking a position as an engineer, sound designer, or music director, for example. An audio portfolio should show diversity and a range of projects. An engineer may want to show work on a rock song, a rap song, a commercial, or other format. The portfolio shows that the engineer can handle effects, reverb, EQ, and balance. It demonstrates that you are able to record a variety of instruments and voices. As you work a job, remember to keep samples of your work for your portfolio. It is good to get copies of

Keeping in Touch

We often shoot off e-mails in such a hurry that we pay them little attention. But you need to take care in the workplace about how you handle them.

- If a work e-mail makes you upset, do not dash off an angry reply and hit send. Take some time to think about what was sent. Are you reading the tone correctly? Is it as serious as it seems? You will have a better reply once you cool down.

- Watch out for humor in an e-mail. Sometimes people do not understand if you are being funny or serious so you have to be aware of possible misinterpretation.

- Use uppercase very judiciously. If you type in all caps, people generally think you are angry.

- Watch who you are replying to. Sometimes you may not notice who has been cc'd on an e-mail. Make sure you know exactly who is seeing your reply to an e-mail. Jobs have been lost when those who were not cautious made comments that were not intended to be seen by a third party.

- Check your Spam folder. Important e-mails occasionally find their way into Spam folders so you should check that folder periodically.

- Do not rely solely on e-mail. If you want to build a professional reputation, you cannot communicate by e-mail alone. You need to pick up the phone and meet with colleagues face to face.

- Do not automatically forward an e-mail. If you intend to forward a work e-mail, check first with the sender. And remember that it

audiotapes as you finish projects and have them ready for future job prospects. Many audio engineers simply put their portfolios online and post MP3s of their work showing the range of sounds. Many engineers have a sampler CD that does the same thing. The artwork is not that important, but as with a résumé, the CD should be clearly labeled with vital information: name, address, phone number. Engineers tend to give notes on how songs were recorded, as well as the techniques and equipment used so prospective employers can have a full picture of the work entailed.

is very easy for others to forward your e-mails as well and that's why it pays to be prudent when writing work messages.

- Make your subject line specific. People want a quick clear snapshot of the content of an e-mail and that's why subject lines are so important. Plus, when you have a concise subject line it is easier to search for information later on.

- Copy the content from the e-mail you are responding to. In general, make sure when you respond to an e-mail that you include the text from the message you are responding to. Often, you can have a long discussion via e-mail but you will lose the thread if previous text does not appear.

- Set up your e-mails to keep copies. Records of your responses can be invaluable. They can show exactly how you handled a situation and when you took action.

- Do not let e-mails be a constant interruption. Some workers respond to e-mail continually throughout the workday. The habit can become a way of procrastinating rather than finishing the tasks that need to be completed.

- Watch your tone of voice. It is very easy to be informal with e-mail communication. But when you are dealing with a client or important corporate communications, you need to be formal and professional. Remember greetings like *Hi*, *Hello* and signoffs like *Regards*, *Sincerely*, and *Thank you*.

Think of Transferable Skills

If you are coming into the recording industry from another field, you should think of skills you do have that will transfer into the recording business. For example, the field is very people-oriented; if you have had a background in customer service, it will serve you well in dealing with recording artists and producers. If you have a sales background, that can help with advertising the services offered at a studio or label, and make it possible for you to bring clients into a studio or convince radio stations to play an artist that you may represent. Organizational skills are highly prized by any company, and in the recording industry a lot of audio information needs to be stored and labeled for easy access. Digital audio tracks may be kept on computers, but still they need to be archived systematically.

Computers play an essential role throughout the recording industry, and those with a history of operating computers and software are valued. Computers are used for recording and mixing using software such as Pro Tools, scheduling artists to record, billing clients, marketing studio services online, and more, so knowing your way around them is vital. If you have a background arranging and scheduling meetings and events, that skill can transfer into the world of recording, where sessions have to be booked and musicians and engineers have to arrive on time with the proper equipment to get the job done. Any experience leading or teaching may be an asset as well since you may find a position directing a team of technicians or coordinating several contributors involved with a musical production. Those with a background in finance also have transferable skills. From record labels to recording studio, accountants and other financial experts can lend their services. Labels need accountants to track expenses for things such as artists' salaries, album marketing, and tours; in addition, they must track profits for things such as tour receipts, CDs, digital downloads, and merchandise. Some accountants may handle payroll as well. In a studio, the accountant monitors income from recording sessions against expenses for staff, rent, maintaining and buying equipment, and other costs.

The Value of Communication

As in many fields, communication skills are crucial when working in the recording industry. As an engineer, you need to be both a good communicator and listener. You need to describe the services you can offer and the vision you may have for an overall sound for a musical act. You also have to be able interpret what an artist may be looking for when they describe the sound they envision.

"You have to be clear and communicate to understand what people want soundwise," says Scott Hull at Masterdisk. "Communication can be one of the most difficult things to teach, and it catches me off guard sometimes. Someone might say something sounds sharp and they may not mean sharp like a note, but brittle or sharp like a knife. Sometimes I have to understand what the producer's vision is and help achieve that. It can be a real challenge when it comes to communication and direction. Sometimes I want to know what a producer's goals are and they don't know themselves."

Hull emphasizes that you have to be honest in the recording business as well. When something sounds bad, you have to find a way to be tactful and communicate that. Hull's clients appreciate his honesty when he tells them he hears something he does not like. Sensitivity and a sense of discretion are needed to gauge just how critical one should be with a client. Many clients have put months of time and effort into a recording, so an engineer cannot be overly critical and point out every flaw. Too much negativity can ruin a career. If you want to be respected in the industry, you have to be able to speak up and explain why something does not sound good and offer suggestions on how the sound can be improved. Through very specific comments, an engineer like Hull can steer clients to thinking in a more productive way about their mix. Although clients may get hurt feelings from criticism of a mix, Hull finds that honesty pays off in the end, and those clients eventually learn to trust Hull's judgment and bring him more work.

Education Advice

There is no set educational background that you need for a job in the recording industry, but there are some overall expectations from employers. At a minimum, many employers want you to have at least a bachelor's degree from a college or university, although many who have specific training from a community college or technical school find employment. If you did not study recording engineering, music, or a topic specifically related to an opening, highlight the college courses that do apply to the position.

As mentioned above, communication is one of the most valued skills in the entertainment business, so if you took English, journalism, writing, public relations, or marketing courses, you may want to point that out. Also, if you worked at a campus radio station, newspaper, or TV station that can be a plus. If you are seeking a specific engineering job, it is helpful to have taken engineering or electrical engineering courses. Internship experience shows that you have worked in a real-life setting and can handle day-to-day tasks.

If you are interested in pursing a higher education focusing on the recording industry, a few schools with programs in this area are San Francisco State University, Arizona Sound Engineering College,

Everyone
Knows

As in most careers, it is the final results of your labors that count. In the recording industry, this means creating an audio piece you can be proud of. But what makes a great recording? If you are trying to create a hit in terms of popular music, you will want your recorded work to have hooks and a memorable chorus. These two music features are the things that stay in people's minds and have them coming back to the music over and over again. You will want your end product to be well produced. Even the hit records made in home studios typically have a professionally produced sound. You will also want your potential hit to be relatively short. The typical radio hit is only between three- and four-and-a-half minutes.

The Art Institute of California–Los Angeles, Kansas City Kansas Community College, Shoreline Community College (Seattle), and Full Sail University (Florida). Technology is always changing in this field, so you should always keep an eye out for professional development classes and adult education classes that will teach you all about cutting edge software, gear, trends, and practices.

Tips for Job Hunting

In a slow economy, job hunters should not put limits on how and where they look for work. You may have a narrow, targeted view of where you would like to work and what position you would like to hold, but when opportunities are limited you are wise to widen your view. Consider possibilities related to your dream job that you may find rewarding. Look beyond your top-10 employers and investigate companies that are connected to your field but may not be a direct match. And when you hear of a job, do not delay. It is a competitive market, and those who apply early have an advantage. Be open to jobs in different locations, although most employment opportunities for audio engineers are in major cities where there are entertainment-related industries: New York City, Los Angeles, Chicago, Seattle, San Francisco, and Atlanta, for example. If you are willing to move, you may be able to find a position that better matches your talents and goals. Plus, certain local economies may be more robust than others.

Check the Help Wanted ads. Although career guru Richard Bolles, author of *What Color Is Your Parachute?* and *The Job-Hunters Survival Guide*, claims that responding to ads is usually not a very effective method for finding work, it still can pay off. Some are still in the newspaper or on a newspaper's Web site. Many ads are listed on specific job sites or in trade and professional journals.

Another good tip for your search is to join a job club. Job clubs are sometimes called networking clubs or job-finding clubs, and they operate as support groups for job hunters. Those who join give each other support and encouragement. Sometimes searching for work on your own can be a lonely endeavor and seekers can lose motivation. Clubs are designed to spur you on. Members exchange job leads, information, and ideas. Bolles claims that job-search support groups have a high success rate of 84 percent. You can try to find one in your area by searching the Internet, the phone book, the Chamber of Commerce, local colleges and universities, and adult education centers, or you can start up your own group with people you know.

Also called career expos, career fairs gather together many employers at a central location, often a convention center. Employers join in career fairs because they are looking to hire and recruit talent. It is an opportunity for you to survey firms and for businesses to discover potential hires. As a job seeker, you go from booth to booth asking questions and gathering information. When you talk to a representative, it can be like a mini job interview. Be sure to bring plenty of résumés with you. While most companies use the fairs as a chance to meet talented individuals, they occasionally hire on the spot. You can find a career fair near you by visiting NationalCareerFairs.com.

Finally, use the Web. There are many top sites for posting your résumé, including Monster.com, CareerBuilder.com, Yahoo! HotJobs, Indeed.com, JobCentral.com, Hound, Career.com, and Simply Hired. Bolles says that you should not rely only on Web sites, because more opportunities turn up in face-to-face conversations. (See Chapter 6 for a list of a few industry-specific job boards worth investigating.)

Here is a list of some of the top broadcast employers:

➡ ABC and Disney (http://corporate.disney.go.com/careers/ index.html) Job openings and a description of the workplace culture are presented here.

➡ CBS (https://sjobs.brassring.com/1033/TG/cim_home.asp ?partnerid=25084&siteid=5129&codes=CBS_Corpmain/ index.aspx) Employment opportunities are listed at CBS along with benefits and a video about CBS.

➡ Lucasfilms (https://jobs.lucasfilm.com/MGM) Search jobs at Lucasfilms and find out about internships and training.

➡ NBC/Universal (http://www.nbcunicareers.com) Explore opportunities at NBC and all its related entertainment branches, including amusement parks.

➡ Paramount (http://www.paramount.com/studio/jobs) Learn about the application process and opportunities offered.

➡ TimeWarner (http://www.timewarner.com/corp/careers) Review career possibilities and submit a résumé online.

➡ Sony (http://www.sony.com/SCA/jobs.shtml) Find out about job positions in the United States and abroad.

➡ Viacom (http://www.viacom.com/careers/Pages/default. aspx) Use the search tools on this site to find positions at Viacom and its related businesses.

➡ Warner Brothers (http://www.warnerbroscareers.com) Find the latest job openings and read the "In the Spotlight" descriptions of positions that need to be filled.

Interviewing Tips

As the old saying goes, first impressions really do count and the interview is your chance to make a good one. If you have not been on a job interview in a while, some of these tips can help you when you go in to meet face-to-face with the person who can hire you.

Before all else, know the details about the position. When you find out about a job opening, find out as much as you can about the job ahead of time so you can explain how your interests and qualifications match the job description. If you have question about the position ahead of time, you may be able to clarify information by phone, speaking to someone in human resources, receptionist, or another person on staff. You want to be as ready as possible to explain how your talents fit the job.

Next, do your homework. Research the establishment that is offering a position. Find out its history, achievement, and plans for the future. This can help you develop intelligent questions to ask during interview and make it easier to explain how you can contribute.

When it comes time for the interview, dress appropriately. Many jobs require you wear a suit and tie and maintain a corporate look, but most jobs in the recording industry are not like that. People working in the recording industry often dress casually, and many even have tattoos and piercings. Even though the dress codes can be loose, when you interview you should still be neat and clean. Do not appear sloppy or wear ill-fitting clothes. You want to convey capability and maturity and how you dress can indicate that. Before you go in for the interview, ask what the overall dress code is. The recording industry is one field where you can actually overdress and come across as "un-hip" and not in tune with the industry.

Always arrive on time. This is one of the biggest factors to making a good first impression. If you arrive late to an interview, it is a strike against you and can cost you getting a job. Every employer wants to hire people who are on time. Always be on the safe side and arrive 10 minutes early. When you do arrive, come prepared. Make sure you have everything with you that you will need. You will always want to carry a copy of your résumé, and you may do well to travel as well with your list of references and copies of any academic transcripts your prospective employer may ultimately want to see. Check if the employer wants to see samples of your work. For an engineering position, the boss may want to hear what you are capable of and you may need to bring an audio portfolio demonstrating the range of your work.

Talk about background that relates to the job. The recording industry is a very creative field and very creative people work in it, so you can bring up elements in your past that demonstrate your interest in music and entertainment. You may have deejayed at a college radio station. You may have an extensive record collection or an interest in a particular band.

As with any interview, be ready for some standard questions. Most interviews cover the same territory and familiar questions. Some of the standards are

➡ *Tell me about yourself.* This is where you go back over your education and applicable job history and mention a bit of your professional goals and why you are there in the first place.

➡ *What's your biggest weakness?* This one comes up often enough and can trip up the interviewee. It is wise to redirect the question and talk about what has been a weakness for you and how you have been working to improve yourself in that particular area. For example, you might say you were not totally familiar with Pro Tools software, but you have been taking time each week to practice on it.

→ *What salary are you looking for?* Salary negotiation is always tricky. You do not want to undervalue yourself and you do not want to price yourself out of a job. Emphasize that you applied because you are interested in the job. That's your first priority and you can come to salary terms once you determine if you are right for the position.

→ *Why should I hire you?* You have to turn on the charm and say how you can really contribute to the company and stress the qualifications that make you the ideal candidate.

At the conclusion of the interview, ask questions. If you have done your research on the company, you will be able to ask intelligent questions about your employer that show you have a true interest in their operations. You can do plenty of research by checking the employer's Web site and searching for information on the Internet. Smart inquiries about the firm's history, products, services, and future goals shows that you are enthusiastic and want to be a part of operations. If you are applying at a recording studio, you may ask about recording projects that you have read about online. How long did the recording take? What type of equipment was used? Were there any unique challenges in recording that act?

Send a follow-up thank-you note to your interviewer. Do not underestimate the power of this gesture. Send one out very soon after the interview to show how prompt and efficient you are. Thank the interviewer for their consideration and again emphasize how much you want the job. If you are offered a job, be willing to start small. If you are trying to enter the recording industry with little experience, expect to take a position with little responsibility and a lot of grunt work. Once you get a foot in the door, you can learn more about the business, prove yourself, and advance.

Résumé Advice

A résumé is still an essential tool for showing your work experience and education. Formats can vary but certain aspects of résumés are universal. It may just be a page, but it has to give a concise snapshot of your work history and help convince an employer that you are the right person for the job.

You do not have to include every job you ever had. You should feature the experience that best applies for the work you are seeking and you usually do not have to show your early jobs as a newspaper boy or babysitter. Some jobs you held may be completely irrelevant so you should leave them off.

Emphasize skills that apply to the job. Each job is unique, but you will want to stress the skills needed for a specific position. For example, if you are applying for an audio engineer job you might list that you have experience with the operation of audio equipment: multi-track soundboards, amplifiers, microphones, loudspeakers, and Pro Tools software. The more varied projects you list the better. It shows you are diversed and can juggle different projects. List whatever experience you have synchronizing, recording, mixing, and reproducing music. You may list some nuts and bolts knowledge of electronics and computers: circuit boards, processors, chips, and the like.

Stress applicable knowledge in your education section. Every résumé will list an applicant's higher education credentials. If you were involved in applicable extracurricular activities, such as working at the school's radio station, you might mention that fact here. You may also list honors and awards. Do not leave out intern or volunteer experience. Even if you did not get paid at a job, if you learned pertinent skills, you will want to list those experiences and the talents you developed.

Consider outside activities and interests. Résumés typically include these interesting items about an applicant's life because they can serve as a "hook," something that intrigues the reader and can be the basis for conversation. You may own every Beatles' album or own a pet iguana. If there is an unusual aspect of your life worth sharing, it can pique interest and conversation on an interview. But don't include it at the expense of keeping your résumé at one, focused page.

Finally, know how to submit your résumé online. Nowadays, most employers will ask you to send in your résumé electronically, attached to an e-mail as a Microsoft Word document. Be sure to label your résumé document so it can be quickly identified. For the file name, put your last name followed by "résumé for [name position]."

Cover Letter

Whether sending in a hard copy résumé or an e-mailed résumé, you will need to write a cover note or letter to go along with it. This is your opportunity to show you have strong communication skills

Everyone
Knows

Computer Essentials

In entering the recording industry, some basic computer knowledge is expected. Many employers expect you to know Windows, Microsoft Word, PowerPoint, and Excel. You might need some familiarity with opening and creating PDFs, depending on the job. Here are a few of the computer basics that many in the recording industry need to know about:

Ableton Live. A professional loop-based software music sequencer for Mac OS and Windows.

Apple Logic Studio. A software package that lets users write, record, edit, and mix their music on Mac computers. Users can add on software such as MainStage, which allows artists to play live loops or prerecorded backing tracks in performance. WaveBurner is a Mac professional application bundled with Logic Studio for assembling, mastering, and burning audio CDs.

Computer music notation software. Helps to desktop-publish musical scores, and makes it easier than writing out music by hand on traditional sheets. Some will write you the score from recorded music.

MIDI (musical instrument digital interface). The industry-standard protocol that enables electronic musical instruments such as keyboard controllers, computers, and other electronic equipment to communicate, control, and synchronize with each other.

Pro Tools software. Pro Tools is a Digital Audio Workstation platform for Mac OS X and Microsoft Windows operating systems. Recording professionals use the software for recording and editing in music production, film scoring, and film and television post production.

Sampling software. Sampling is the act of taking a piece of music and reusing it in recording a new song or as its own instrument. Some artists sample a snatch of music and repeat it in a loop.

Sequencer. In digital audio recording, a sequencer is a computer program or a program in a stand-alone keyboard that puts together a sound sequence from a series (or sequence) of musical instrument digital interface (MIDI) events (operations). The MIDI sequencer does not record the actual audio, but rather the events related to the performance. So after you record a piece with a piano sound, you can change the sound to an organ sound at the touch of a button because you have the sequence of the music recorded.

and can write in a professional manner, that you are not prone to typos, misspellings, or grammatical mistakes. Here you can give a quick sense of who you are as a person. You might convey that you are a serious worker but you have a positive attitude and a sense of humor. In the letter, you identify the job you are applying for and possibly how you heard about the job. You say who you are and give a sense of the experience you have had that makes you right for the position. Explain why the company should be interested in you. For example, you have operated a home studio for several years and produced a couple independent albums that have garnered critical notice. Or you have been working in public relations and aim to apply the skills you acquired to a job within the communications department of a major label.

All a cover letter needs is an introduction, one to three paragraphs of text, and a short wrap-up paragraph suggesting the next course of action (e.g., "I will contact you in a few days to follow up.") You may impress by showing you have done some research on the firm. If you are entering the field with little direct experience, you will need to stress your applicable and transferable skills, and highlight why you would still be right for the position. Even though your contact information should be on your résumé, make sure as a precaution that it is on your cover letter as well.

References and Letters of Recommendation

If an employer is seriously considering you as a job candidate, he or she will want to contact references and perhaps see letters of recommendation. Generally, you need three to five references—people who are willing to endorse you as a worker and can speak about your prior experience. You usually present your references on a prepared list that is not your résumé. The list needs to include reference names, title, and contact information. Remember, these are professionals who can vouch for your professionalism so you usually do not list friends or family members. Be sure that your references know they are your references! Tell them what jobs you are applying for and that they might be contacted by an employer. You can coach the reference in advance as well. If you are applying for a music publicist position, tell your reference to play up your communication skills and any related experience.

Chapter 5

Talk Like a Pro

There are many phrases, slang terms, abbreviations, and technical terms that someone working in the recording industry should know. Even if you have been in the industry a few years, there are a wealth of terms related to technical aspects, publishing, and music performance that you have yet to learn. Knowing the jargon can help further establish your reputation as a professional, so take a thorough look at the words and definitions in this chapter. There are many other recording industry terms in additions to these, but the entries here are among some of the most important.

A&R (artists and repertoire) The record company department that is dedicated to finding new singers, bands, etc. to record.

AAC Advanced Audio Coding is an MP4 file format.

absorption The dissipation of sound waves as they interact with matter. According to the book *Recording Studio Design* by Phillip Newell, absorption is the most important controlling factor in room acoustics.

AC The abbreviation for alternating current, an electrical current that flows back and forth in a circuit, and the type of current that supplies all our electricity today.

acoustics The science of sound.

A/D Short for analog-digital conversion.

add A song that gets added to a playlist at a radio station.

advance   A record label will sometimes give an artist money in advance that has to be paid back over time from royalties earned and album sales.

airplay   Broadcast of a song on radio.

album   A collection of songs in a recorded format, either on CD, vinyl, cassette, or digital downloads.

ambient sound   Sound that comes from the surrounding environment instead of the intended sound source.

ampere   A unit of current; called an amp in its shortened form.

amplification   An amount of increase in signal power, voltage, or current.

amplitude   A measure of the amount of energy in a sound wave.

analog   An analog signal is continuous. Audiophiles say that with analog recording, the sound wave form most resembles the sound wave of the original source. Phonograph records or vinyl and magnetic tapes are the means to store the continual audio waves captured in analog recording.

analog to digital converter   A device that translates analog recording into digital data.

Apple Logic Studio   A software package that lets users write, record, edit, and mix their music on Mac computers. Users can add on software such as MainStage, which allows artists to play live loops or prerecorded backing tracks in performance. WaveBurner is a professional application bundled with Apple Logic Studio for assembling, mastering, and burning audio CDs.

attack   The rate at which sound starts and rises in volume.

Audio Interchange File Format (AIFF)   Digital audio file format used by Apple. These files are uncompressed and quite large compared to MP3s.

author   A songwriter. A copyright of a song is split between two parties: the author and the publisher.

auxiliary equipment   Sound effects units that are separate from the main recording console but can be added to it to provide different sounds and alterations to sounds.

background noise   The noise in a system when there is no signal present.

baffles   Sound absorbing panels that can be moved and prevent certain sound waves from entering or leaving a space. Often baffles are put around drums to contain the sound and get a more closely miked sound.

balance control The dial that allows the user to shift the sound in a stereo amplifier from right to left speakers or vice versa.

band In audio engineering terms this means a range of frequencies.

bandwidth This is the width of a range of frequencies that an electronic device uses, stated in terms of the difference between the lowest and highest frequencies.

bar code The Universal Product Code (UPC) code (black and white bars and numbers that you see on packages) that identifies a product for computer tracking. All CDs have a distinct bar code.

bass The lower range of frequencies or the stringed instrument that plays lower range notes.

beat A succession of strokes on a drum or other percussion instrument that can be altered according to speed or number.

beats A sequence of individual beats.

bit The smallest unit of digital information expressed as either a 0 or a 1.

blanket license A performing rights organization will issue a blanket license that makes it possible for radio and television stations, DJs, musicians, and public businesses to play music without having to acquire rights each time they play a song.

book a session To schedule recording time.

boombox A portable stereo system popular for playing music outdoors on city streets, beaches, etc. Popular among break dancers.

boomstand A vertical stand with telescoping attachment to hold a microphone, like the boom in nautical terms, which is a long spar extending from the mast to hold the sail.

boost Increasing the gain using the equalizer.

bootleg An illegal recording (CD, DVD, etc.) sold outside the normal legal channels. The sellers of this music are often called pirates.

break A record label will "break" an artist, meaning they get the act enough airplay and media attention that they start to become popular on a national level, translating into significant album and song sales.

break-even point When a record label brings in enough revenue from an album to recoup all expenses, it has hit the break-even point. Any revenue surpassing expense is profit.

burn A common term for making a copy of a CD off a computer.

buss/bus   A wire that is feeding into one or more track outputs of the console.

cable assembly   A wire or set of wires that are terminated at the ends with contacts and connectors to establish an electrical connection between two points.

cans   Slang for headphones.

CD   Short for compact disc, an optical disc with digital sound information recorded on it or intended for recording.

CD-ROM   A compact disc that can store a large amount of digital data and be read by a computer.

channel   A path that the audio signal travels along from the source to the recording device. It is not unusual to hear in a recording studio a phrase such as "I've got the guitar in channel one." Most likely the engineer is recording that single channel onto a single track of a multitrack recording device.

chops   Slang for the ability to play an instrument.

chorus   The section of a song that is repeated and has the same lyrics. It is usually the hook of the song that most people can sing back and remember. Chorus also can mean a group of many singers or an effect that simulates a vocal chorus.

click track   Generally, the click track is an electronic metronome fed into the headphones of the musician so they can stay with the beat when recording. Drummers often rely on a click track so they do not slow down or speed up.

clip   An audio system has an upper level beyond which the sound level will not go. On a mixing board this is when the volume goes way into the red and the sound distorts. It clips off the top of the waveform.

close miking   Placing a microphone close to the source so it picks up mostly that sound and little ambient noise.

compression   Compression can have two meanings in today's recording industry. In recording or broadcasting, it is a control to reduce the dynamic range of an audio signal. Compression is applied to make both the soft and loud parts of a sound more tolerable at the same volume setting. The term compression can also apply to the process of encoding digital audio data so it takes up less space. An MP3 is an example of digital audio compression.

compulsory mechanical license   This rule lets anyone record and distribute any commercially released, non-dramatic song as long as the mechanical license rates are paid to the copyright owner of the song.

console   Also called the mixing console or board. This is the command center for the recording engineer used for recording sound and controlling it.

controlled composition   A song that is written and owned by the recording artist.

control room   The room where the engineer and producer oversee the production of a recording.

copyright   Exclusive ownership and right to reproduce, publish, sell, and distribute a work granted to the creator. In the recording industry, the matter is a song. The law automatically grants a copyright once a song is recorded in some tangible form such as on a hard disc, CD, tape, or even a piece of paper. When it comes to broadcasting, U.S. copyright law sets the payment rate at 9.1¢ per play.

Copyright Office   A part of the Library of Congress that issues copyrights, a form of legal protection on intellectual property such as music or writing.

Copyright Royalty Board (CRB)   The CRB makes decisions involving the adjustment of copyright royalty rates as well as the terms and payments of royalties that fall under copyright laws.

creative control   Also called artistic control, this is a term used to describe the authority of having final creative say over a project. Sometimes a recording artist will not want a producer to have final say over how an album should sound. That artist will want to maintain creative control.

cross-collateralization   This practice allows one party to recover advances via funds earned from another source. For example, a record label may use the practice to collect royalties on an album that sells well to repay the losses on a previous album that sold poorly.

cue sheet   Detailed timing information for a film or television program indicating musical works used and durations of each musical piece. The cue sheet is used for royalty collection purposes. The term is also used to describe a list of mixer control adjustments that need to be made in the final mixdown of a recording.

cylinder   The earliest recordings made by Thomas Alva Edison in the late 1800s were made and played back on a cylinder. His cylinder players were called phonographs.

D/A   Short for digital-analog conversion, translating digital data number in the continuous analog waveform.

damping   Decreasing the vibration. A studio engineer may want to damp the snare to get rid of a bit of a ringing sound.

DAT   Short for digital audio tape, DAT is standard format for recording digitally. Recorded data goes on to a small specially designed cassette tape.

DAW   Short for digital audio workstation.

deaden   To limit or muffle the sound. A dead space is very sound absorbent.

decay   The time period from when an audio signal's peak level drops down to a sustain level or the fade-out rate of a reverberating sound.

decibel (dB)   A unit used to measure the power of a signal, such as an electrical signal or sound.

decks   Turntables used by deejays in conjunction with a mixer are often called decks.

de-esser   An audio device (compressor or limiter) that reduces the annoying sound of the spoken or sung "S."

degauss   To degrease or eliminate an unwanted magnetic field; a process used to remove any previously written data on a tape or other magnetized storage device.

delay effects   Echo, reverb delay, flanging, and chorusing are types of delay effects. They delay a signal for the original source using a recording or delay device.

demo   This is a recording that an artist or band uses to demonstrate their sound and songwriting. Artists use it to try to land a deal with a label, manager, publisher, or agent. Usually it is made for little money to give the listener idea of the song, performance skills, and talents of the artist.

derivative work   A new work of music established from one or more pre-existing pieces of music.

development deal   When a music publisher finances the quality studio recordings of an album in exchange for royalty payments or the rights to sell or license the recordings in exchange for royalties or a percentage of profits. A development deal can also be when a record company pays for a producer to record an act, and, in return, the label may get first refusal. If the label likes what it hears, it may then sign the act to a record deal.

diamond   In terms of album sales, diamond means 10 million albums sold at wholesale, according to the Recording Industry Association of America.

diaphragm   A thin piece of material (such as paper, plastic or aluminum) inside a microphone which vibrates when it is struck by sound waves; these vibrations are converted into an electrical current which becomes the audio signal.

diffusion   The even distribution of sound in a room.

digipak   A popular proprietary type of CD and DVD packaging.

digital performance of sound recordings   This is a relatively new concept that defines the digital audio transmission of a recorded work via the Internet or satellite broadcast. It does not cover broadcast by the traditional "terrestrial broadcasters"— radio and televisions stations (although they may be using a digital broadcast system).

digital recording   The process of making audio signals into a numeric digital sequence and storing this information.

digital rights management (DRM)   Access control technologies that impose limitations on use of digital content and devices in order to prevent unauthorized duplication of a work.

direct box   Direct boxes are often used to plug an instrument directly into a sound board in a live performance situation. The device translates instrument-level output to a balanced, low-impedance mike-level output.

direct interjection or direct input (DI)   The miking process of taking an audio signal from an electrical instrument and directly feeding it into a mixing board, often through a direct box. This can be used as a substitute to placing a microphone in front of an amplifier in live situations. Sometimes this is also called direct pick-up.

disc/disk   Many people use the words interchangeably to refer to compact discs and CD-ROMs. But in the late-19th century and into the twentieth century, the word disc was used to refer to phonograph records. When engineers developed data storage devices, they decided to use the "k" spelling of disk. Some say discs are optical media like CDs, CD-ROMs, and DVDs, and disks are magnetic like a floppy disk or the disk in a computer hard drive.

disc jockey   Also known as a deejay or DJ, this professional plays the music at a radio station and speaks during music breaks, offering information, jokes, news, etc.

distant miking   Placing a microphone far from the source when recording.

distortion   A change to the expected wavelength form of an audio signal. A guitarist may purposely cause audio distortion by overloading an amplifier.

DIY   Short for do it yourself and referred to in the music business as making, distributing, and selling your own albums.

Dolby   The manufacturer brand name of a popular noise reduction system that improves the fidelity of audio recording, playback, and broadcast.

door   The amount of money collected from audience members who pay to see a show. Musical acts who are just starting out play for the door or more likely, a percentage of the door.

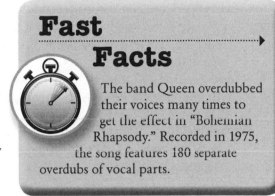

Fast Facts

The band Queen overdubbed their voices many times to get the effect in "Bohemian Rhapsody." Recorded in 1975, the song features 180 separate overdubs of vocal parts.

dropout   The short disappearance of audio signal during recording.

drum booth/drum room   A special isolation chamber used for recording drums in some studios.

drum machine   A synthesizer that can mimic different drum sounds and play back drum patterns.

dubbing   The process of making copies of recorded music. Sometimes it refers to editing a recorded sound and editing it together with another recording.

duplication   Replicating a CD.

dynamics   The amount of change in loudness and softness of audio levels in a piece of music.

echo   A distinct repeat of sound that follows the original sound. Sometimes mistakenly used when reverberation is meant.

editing   Putting together sequences of a recording or replacing already recorded tracks on a multitrack recording with new recorded segments.

effects   Methods that modify the audio signal, such as echo, distortion, and reverb. The term can be short for sound effects as well, such as a door slamming, a gunshot, howling wind, footsteps, etc.

eight-track tape An audio tape format created by Lear and made popular in the 1970s until the advent of cassette tapes.

EQ This is a shorthand term for equalization, which is the adjustment of various frequency components of sound (through filtering and amplification).

evergreen In the recording industry, this is the term for a song that gets recorded and performed by artists for many years, such as "Yesterday" by the Beatles or "Louie, Louie" by the Kingsmen.

fade A gradual reduction of sound. Many songs fade out rather than end cold. Few songs fade in, although the Beatles "Eight Days a Week" and "Bittersweet Symphony" by the Verve fade in, whereas "Hey, Jude" by the Beatles and "Born to be Wild" by Steppenwolf fade out. In fact, "Hey Jude" takes a full two minutes to fade out.

feed To send an audio signal, or a general term for the electronic distribution of text, audio, or video.

feedback The howling sound heard when a sound loop is created between an audio input like a microphone or guitar pickup and an audio output like a loudspeaker.

fidelity The quality of a recording or reproduction. For example, high fidelity means a recording that has reproduced sound as close to the original source as possible.

file sharing Distributing or offering access to digitally stored information.

filter An audio filter removes sound signals with frequencies above or below a certain level.

fixed in the tangible medium of expression A copyright term that means a work has a valid copyright as soon as recorded or written down in a manner that is sufficiently permanent.

flange An audio effect creating modulated short delays of direct signal.

flutter High-frequency variations in pitch, caused by speed changed in a recorder.

frequency Sound is created when an object vibrates. Frequency is a measurement of sound waves. It is the number of sound waves that pass a point each second. Frequency is directly related to pitch.

gain Gain can be a term used for the overall amount of volume. On an amplifier, gain is the volume to the preamp section. Volume turns up the power amp section.

gate A noise gate is an electronic device or software logic used to control an audio signal's volume. It is used in recording and live sound to control the volume level of any audio signal.

generation A term used to describe the number of times that a recording has been copied.

generation loss With every copy generation of a recording, sound quality deteriorates. This is called generation loss.

graphophone A cylinder-playing audio device invented by Charles Tainter and Chinchester Bell in the 1880s. It competed with Thomas Alva Edison's phonograph.

hard disk recording Digital audio recording directly onto a hard disk.

harmonic An overtone, secondary tone that is higher than the primary or fundamental tone.

high end Frequencies that are pitched high. Certain very high frequencies may only be heard by dogs and other animals.

hot When the recording signal is too high.

hum 60 Hz power line current accidentally induced or fed into electronic equipment causes a hum.

Hz Short for Hertz, which is a unit of frequency.

impedance A material's resistance to the flow of electrical current, measured in Ohms. Impedance can affect the way a loudspeaker sounds because of frequency response and controlling the motion of the loudspeaker cone.

input A jack or the location where a device physically receives an audio signal.

isolation booth/isolation room A room that blocks sounds from outside from leaking in.

iTunes This popular digital media application from Apple is designed for playing and organizing digital audio and media files.

jack An input on a console, amplifier, or other device where you feed in or out the audio signal.

jewel case The standard plastic CD case.

joint work According to copyright laws, a work created by two or more people.

lead sheet A written chart indicating the melody, lyrics, and chords of a tune. It features full musical notation.

leakage When a microphone recording one instrument picks up sounds from other instruments and sources that were not intended to be recorded by that microphone.

level In audio engineering, a level is usually a measure of amplitude.

license In the music industry, this is permission to use a recording for a particular purpose, as part of television show or movie soundtrack, for example.

limiter A device that decreases gain when input voltage rises above a certain level.

line A recording studio term for a cable.

line level A signal level from an amplifier, used as the normal level that carries through the interconnecting cables in a control room.

lockout A secure, uninterrupted recording session. A studio may book a week lockout session with a musical act where the studio dedicates all its time to recording that act and no one else.

logging The tracking of individual songs broadcast. Radio stations maintain detailed logging of songs played.

loop A continual repeat of a sound.

low-end The deep bass frequencies.

LP The popular abbreviation for a long-playing record album.

magnetic tape Recording tape consisting of a plastic strip to which magnetic materials, often finely ground iron oxide particles, adheres.

majors, the The shorthand terms for the four major recording/entertainment conglomerates. The Big Four are the Universal Music Group (UMG), Sony BMG Music Entertainment, Bertelsmann, and the Warner Music Group.

master As a noun, master is the original recording made in the studio from which all copies should be made.

mastering Mastering is the final engineering stage in an audio recording. Mastering adjusts the final sound to meet industry standards of quality.

mechanical royalties These are royalties paid to the copyright owner of a song whenever the song is reproduced. These are payments made for the reproduction of songs on CD, vinyl, musical greeting cards, and other formats. The Copyright Royalty Board sets the rates. The recording artist may also receive mechanical royalties depending on their deal with a record label.

meter A gauge that measures audio signals.

mic An abbreviation for microphone.

microphone An instrument used to pick up sound waves for broadcast, recording, or amplification.

MIDI (musical instrument digital interface)   A method
of communication between computers, mixers, musical
instruments, and accessories. The system uses a set of messages
that can represent musical performance, mixing movements, or
other data. If a keyboard is hooked to a computer, using MIDI, a
computer-sequencing program is capable of recording a musical
performance.

mixing   This is the recording engineer's art of putting together
recorded musical and audio information to create one whole
piece of music. Engineers mix together different tracks from a
multitrack recording to make one final audio work.

mixing console   The instrument used to combine all the recorded
tracks into a one final recorded work.

modulation   A process of varying one waveform in relation to
another waveform, used to send an information-bearing signal
over long distances.

monitor   As a verb, monitor means to listen. On stage, the
monitors are speakers that allow a band to hear themselves
during performance. In a recording studio, monitor speakers are
specifically built for mixing and mastering. The concept behind
these speakers is to give engineers a sound that will let them
mix tracks that will sound good on any playback system—a car
radio, stereo, boombox, etc.

MP3   MP3 stands for MPEG-1, Audio Layer-3. MPEG itself stands
for Motion Pictures Expert Group, which sets standards for
audio and video compression and transmission. This popular
digital audio format allows the user to compress audio data.
MP3 files can be easily downloaded online through computers
and listened to on digital music players.

MP4   MP4 stands for MPEG-1, Audio Layer-4. It is a file format
used primarily to compress video files.

multitrack recording   This idea of recording different
instruments of different tracks really is the foundation of modern
recording where instruments are recorded on separate tracks
and then an engineer or producer "mixes" the tracks together
to make the desired overall song or sound. Les Paul is generally
credited with making the first multitrack recording around 1947.

mute button   This switch takes out a track signal when listening
back to a recording in the monitors.

music publisher   An entity that takes care of the business
administration of a song—seeking out opportunities for it to

be performed or licensed for use in television shows and films, for example. Songwriters can be their own publishers or they can strike deals to give publishing rights to established music publishers.

Nielsen SoundScan   This company collects sales information from UPC bar code scanners, in order to determine the number of CDs sold.

noise reduction   Any instrument that removes noise from a recording system.

OGG Vorbis   A file format that is an audio codec that is open source and free, frequently used in video games.

Ohm   A unit measuring the opposition to electrical current flow.

one sheet   A single piece of paper highlighting all the essential details of a record release.

oscilloscope   A device that pictures sound waves.

overdub   To add more musical parts to a preexisting multitrack recording. A band may record basic tracks of guitar, bass, drums, and vocal and then overdub keyboards, percussion, and any other instruments.

P2P   A system of networking computers over the Internet to exchange files directly, or peer-to-peer. The record industry has said that P2P has led to illegal music file sharing.

patch   To direct or redirect the signal in an audio system like a console.

patch cord   A cable with two plug endings that connects two jacks to direct audio signals.

peak   The highest point in an audio waveform.

performing rights license   A performing rights organization often authorizes the public performance of a song through a blanket rights license.

performing rights organization (PRO)   A group that serves as an intermediary between copyright holders and those who wish to use copyrighted works. ASCAP, BMI, and SESAC are the big three PROs.

phase   A measurement of the time difference between similar waveforms.

phase shifter   An audio effects device that introduces a delay into an audio signal to create an audio distortion.

phonograph   A name used to described a common device for playing recorded music from the 1870s until today. (*Phonograph* is another term for record player or turntable.)

pickup   A device in an electrical guitar that allows for the transmission of the instrument's sound into an amplifier, console, etc.

piracy   Illegally reproducing sound recordings for distribution and/or sale.

pitch   There are two distinct meanings for the word pitch. It can mean to attempt selling a song to a music publisher or producer, but in music, pitch is how high or low a sound seems.

platinum   The designation for selling 1 million copies of an album, according RIAA. An album selling at least 2 million copies is called double-platinum or multi-platinum.

playback   The process of playing (and listening) to audio tracks have been recorded.

playlist   In a recording studio, the playlist is the series of commands given to a computer on how to play back digital audio files—which tracks get played, at which levels, etc. At a radio station, the playlist is the list of songs that the disc jockey plays during his or her show.

polarity   The direction of current flow or magnetic force.

power amplifier   A power amplifier supplies current to speakers. The power amplifier delivers a high power signal necessary to drive the speakers to the desired output level.

preamplifier   Often called a *preamp*, this device enhances sound quality. The preamp helps increase the power and sound of the main amplifier or power amp. In the typical audio system, a preamplifier only provides a voltage gain. The preamplifier does not provide current. The second amplifier, which is called the power amplifier, delivers the necessary current to the speakers.

preview   In the recording studio, this is the process of listening back to an audio track before committing to save it.

production   The actual process of recording music.

promo   A copy of a record given away in order to promote a musical act.

Pro Tools   Pro Tools is a digital audio workstation platform for Mac OS X and Microsoft Windows operating systems. Recording professionals use the software for recording and editing in music production, film scoring, and in film and television post-production.

receiver   The receiving end of a communications channel. In audio terms, it usually refers to a radio receiver that receives signals broadcast by radio broadcast systems.

recording session   The period of time when recording is actually taking place.

reverb   An audio effect that makes a persistence of a sound after it has been played.

rhythm tracks   Generally, this is a recording of the bass and drums. An engineer may record the rhythm tracks first to get a solid foundation for the rest of the recording.

rider   This is an attachment to a contract that adds on specified terms. It is used often for concert contracts. The riders may give specific conditions that are set forth by an artist and must be met by a venue. The rider can give specific demands about lighting, sound equipment, stage size, and other technical aspects. It can also detail more minor elements, such as the type of food the artist needs to have back stage.

Fast Facts

While songwriters and publishers currently collect royalties for the broadcast of their songs, performers do not get paid. Jack Ely sings on one of the most well-known versions of "Louie, Louie," a song he recorded with the Kingsmen in 1963. Although the song continues to get steady play on oldies radio stations and in stadiums, he does not receive a dime. The children of the songwriter, Richard Berry, however, receive about $100,000 in royalties every year. A bill wending its way through Congress in 2009 is designed to change that and provide compensation for the performers, but as of this printing, the law has not passed. In the 1990s, the recording industry won the right to collect royalties for performers when songs are played on satellite, Internet, and cable radio.

riff   A short melody, often played on guitar, that repeats throughout a song and may serve as a hook.

rotation   Groups of recordings that are played within a certain period of time at a radio station. The goal of most recording artists is to get into "heavy rotation."

rough mix   An engineer will generally make a rough mix of song before committing. Members of a band and the producer listen to the rough mix and then suggest changes and overdubs.

royalties   Payments collected from the use of music, whether the music is broadcast, performed, sold, or used in another manner. Songwriters and publishers, for example, collect royalties when songs are broadcast.

runching in and out   When a musician or singer makes a mistake or is not satisfied with a part in a multitrack recording, the artist can go back to the exact spot and the engineer can hit the record button at the exact point that a fix is needed. Sometimes an engineer will punch in a single word or note to make a recording sound better.

sampling   Sampling is the act of taking a piece of music and reusing it in recording a new song or as its own instrument.

scratch vocals   A vocal performance that the other players in a band hear as they record their tracks but that are not the final vocal performance in a recording.

sequencer   In digital audio recording, a sequencer is a computer program or a program in a stand-alone keyboard that puts together a sound sequence from a series (or sequence) of Musical Instrument Digital Interface (MIDI) events (operations). The MIDI sequencer does not record the actual audio, but rather the events related to the performance. So after you record a piece with a piano sound, you can change the sound to an organ sound at the touch of a button because you have the sequence of the music recorded.

signal-to-noise ratio   Abbreviated as S/N, this ratio is the level of an audio signal compared to the level of noise in a system, which can corrupt the audio signal. In layman's terms, this is a measure of the sound of the music to the background noise. The higher the ratio, the less the background noise interferes.

SoundExchange   An organization created by the RIAA to collect royalties on the digital performance of sound recordings. For example, SoundExchange negotiates royalty payments with Internet radio stations.

SRLP (suggested retail list price)   The approximate price received by a retailer for selling a recording. Traditionally, an artist would receive a royalty based on these sales figures.

statutory rate   Set by the U.S. Congress, this amount is how much writers/publishers receive for the mechanical royalties. The rate changes with the economy and was recently $.08 for songs five minutes and under. Record labels sometimes negotiate a lower statutory rate.

sweetening   Adding musical parts to a recording to make it sound better, especially melodic instruments such as strings and/or horns.

synchronization rights   When a song is used in a movie, television show, or commercial, producers have to get a synchronization license and pay a fee for synchronization rights.

take   In a recording studio, a take is each performance that is recorded. You will often hear an engineer say, "Take 1" or "Take 2."

take sheet   A chart for keeping track of each take and jotting notes about each one. An engineer may mark on the take sheet which takes sounded best so he or she can go back and retrieve it when doing a mix.

talkback   The intercom that allows for communication between the engineer in the control room and the musicians in the studio room.

tapeless studio   A recording studio that relies solely on a digital recording system.

tempo   The speed of the music. Songs can have a fast, slow, or medium tempo.

thin sound   When the sound is lacking frequencies, especially a deficiency in low frequencies.

time code   The abbreviated phrase for the SMPTE Time Code (Society of Motion Picture and Television Engineers Time Code). This is a standardized timing and sync signal used in film and television programming.

tone   Sound quality.

track   A recording of one distinct instrument or voice. Multitrack recording has made it possible to combine different single tracks to make a complete recorded song.

track log/track assignment sheet   A chart used by the engineer to know exactly what information is recorded on each track of a recording.

trades   This is short for trade magazines. In the recording and music industry, the big trades magazines are *Billboard, Radio & Records, Pollstar, Broadcasting and Cable,* and *Variety.*

transcription license   Permission to make a recording of a song as long as it is not for future sale or distribution to the public. Radio stations use this license when getting the rights to use music as part of radio commercials.

transpose   Changing the musical key of an entire piece of music up or down by a constant interval.

tray   The part of a CD case where the CD sits.

tray card   The artwork for a CD that slides into the front of the jewel case.

tremolo   An effect created by the rapid repetition of a single note. It has a wavering quality.

trim control   A device that lowers signal strength in an amplifier—often it rises into a restricted range.

turntable   A term for a record player or phonograph that plays records.

tweak   Slightly adjusting the calibration or setting of operating controls for best performance.

tweeter   A loudspeaker or part of a speaker that reproduces higher-frequency sounds.

vamp   In a musical performance, repeating part of the tune over and over at the end, often ending in a fade.

vibrato   Smooth repeated changing of pitch.

vocal booth   An isolation booth specifically for recording the voice.

voice over   Recording of the words spoken by an announcer who reads text for a radio or television commercial.

volt   A unit of electric potential or electromotive force.

volume   A term used to describe a level of loudness.

vox   An abbreviation used for voice, usually used when keeping the track log.

watermarking   Adding a code to digital data files as a means of labeling or recognizing them.

watt   A unit of electric power.

WAV   Generally, a digital file of uncompressed audio; a universally accepted file format for source audio.

waveform   A graph of an audio signal's sound pressure or voltage over time.

WMA   Windows Media Audio, the proprietary digital audio file format from Microsoft.

woofer   A loudspeaker or part of a speaker that reproduces the lower bass frequencies only.

Chapter 6

Resources

Associations and Organizations

American Society of Composers and Publishers (ASCAP) A performing rights association for composers, songwriters, lyricists, and music publishers of every kind of music. ASCAP licenses music and distributes royalties for performance or broadcast of copyrighted works.   (http://www.ascap.com)

Artistshouse Music This nonprofit, online organization gives informational support, guidance, and expert resources to help navigate challenges and maximize opportunities in the music industry. (http://www.artistshousemusic.org)

Association for Multimedia Communications An organization dedicated to advancing the professional concerns of multimedia specialists. The group is for people who work on the Web, CD-ROMs and DVDs, interactive kiosks, streaming media, or other digital forms. The AMC promotes understanding of technology, e-learning, and e-business, and helps members achieve success through education and networking.   (http://www.amcom.org)

Audio Engineering Society Engineers, scientists, manufacturers, students, and other individuals who are interested in the professional audio technology belong to this group to share information, network, and promote standards.   (http://www.aes.org)

Broadcast Music, Inc. A performing rights association that collects license fees on behalf of its songwriters, composers, and music publishers and distributes them as royalties.   (http://www.bmi.com)

Game Audio Network Guild This group supports career development for game audio professionals, publishers, developers, and students. While the site does not offer job listings, it does promote job networking. The guild presents informative panels and online resources, updated regularly, featuring conversations on contracts, negotiations, basic business skills, and deal points, as well as information on creative and technical issues.   (http://www.audiogang.org)

Graphic Artists Guild A professional organization that can provide career information for multimedia developers.   (http://www.gag.org)

Music and Film Industry Association of America This is the organization that was formed when the Motion Picture Association of America, Inc. (MPAA) and the Recording Industry Association of America (RIAA) merged in 2006. The two organizations have very similar goals for fighting piracy, from bootlegged product to illegal downloads.   (http://mafiaa.org)

National Association of Music Merchants This organization represents the global music products industry and works to increase active participation in music making.   (http://www.namm.org)

National Association of Record Industry Professionals This association was formed to promote education, career advancement, and good will among record executives. Its Web site features information on industry trends and news that anyone in the industry may find of interest.   (http://www.narip.com)

National Association of Recording Merchandisers The association serves the music content delivery community in a variety of areas including networking, advocacy, information, education, and promotion. Members are music wholesalers and retailers, as well as online and mobile music delivery companies.   (http://www.narm.com)

The Recording Academy The group that organizes the Grammy awards which recognizes the best in recorded music each year. Grammy.com has its Producers and Engineers Wing, which is comprised of producers, engineers, remixers, manufacturers, technologists, and other related music recording industry professionals. This branch addresses critical issues that affect the art and craft of recorded music.   (http://www.grammy.com)

Recording Industry Association of America This trade group, which represents the recording industry, works to protect intellectual property rights, conducts research on the industry, and monitors and reviews state and federal laws and regulations influencing the recording business. To qualify for membership, you must work at a major or independent label, record distributor, or a record marketing or personal management firm. Lawyers, publicists, and consultants whose main client base is the record business are also welcome.   (http://www.riaa.com)

SESAC Originally called the Society of European Stage Authors and Composers when it was formed in 1930, SESAC is simply known by its letters today. It is the smallest of the three performing rights organizations. (ASCAP and BMI are the other two bigger groups.). SESAC became affiliated with many gospel recordings, and their roster includes Bob Dylan, Neil Diamond, Rush, and many other artists.   (http://www.sesac.com)

Society of Professional Audio Recording Services This group holds conferences and publishes papers about the professional audio community. Its members include many of the top audio engineers working in the industry today.   (http://www.spars.com)

Books and Periodicals

Books

Books: Industry Overview

100 Careers in the Music Business. By Tanja L. Crouch (Barron's, 2008). This book gives profiles on 100 different music-related occupations. Learn about the duties and necessary qualifications, as well as the roles of music publishers, recording companies, record distribution groups, the musicians, producers, management teams, and marketing and promotion operations.

All You Need to Know About the Music Business. By Donald Passman (Free Press, 2006). Passman sets out to give musicians, performers, and songwriters the tools to hire advisers, market their careers, protect their creative works, and generally cope with a complex industry in a state of flux.

Assistant Engineer Handbook: Gigs in the Recording Studio and Beyond. By Sarah Jones (Schirmer Trade Books, 2004). This is a complete reference for technical careers in the recording studio.

The Business of Audio Engineering. By Dave Hampton (Hal Leonard Music Pro Guides Series, 2008). This book is about the professional life of the audio engineer, with business strategies, from attracting clients to keeping them, from hiring studios to working on your own, from dealing with problem artists, producers and labels to handling a crisis and getting paid what you are worth.

This Business of Music, 10th Edition. By M. William Krasilovsky and Sidney Shemel (Watson-Guptill Publications, 2007). This is considered one of the bibles of the music business, and it gives nuts and bolts information on standard contract provisions, copyrights, ownership, technical jargon, and the historical context for many industry practices. It is regarded as a standard reference book for all music professionals.

The Future of the Music Business: How to Succeed with the New Digital Technologies, 2nd Edition. By Steve Gordon (Hal Leonard Books, 2008). Learn to sell music online, develop an online record company, create an Internet radio station, open an online music store, use peer-to-peer networks to promote and sell music, and take advantage of wireless technologies.

How to Be a Record Producer in the Digital Era. By Megan Perry (Billboard Books, 2008). This book is well-suited to people who have recorded a few bands and now want to advance their careers. Gives good basic information about how to run a recording session, manage a budget, and deal with copyrights and contracts. It is a comprehensive look at the technical and business sides of producing.

Music, Money and Success: The Insider's Guide to Making Money in the Music Industry, 5th Edition. By Todd Brabec and Jeff Brabec (Schirmer Trade Books, 2006). The fifth edition covers negotiations and the money that can be made from practically every area of music for songwriters, composers, and music publishers. This edition covers topics such as download and streaming royalties; ringtone, ringback, and master tone cell phone royalties; and video game licenses and royalties.

The Recording Industry. By Geoffrey Hull (Routledge, 2004). This is a comprehensive examination of how records are made, marketed, and sold.

What They'll Never Tell You About the Music Business: The Myths, Secrets, Lies (& a Few Truths). By Peter M. Thall (Billboard Books, 2007). An insider's guide that provides details on recording agreements, record royalties, artistic management, music publishing, music marketing and promotion, merchandising, copyright infringement, and the international music business scene.

Books: History of the Industry

America on the Record: A History of Recorded Sound. By Andre Millard (Press Syndicate of the University of Cambridge, 1996). This book provides a history of sound recording from the first sheet of tinfoil that was manipulated into retaining sound to the high-tech digital world. This book examines the important technical developments of acoustic, electric, and digital sound reproduction while outlining the cultural impact of recorded music and movies.

Appetite for Self-Destruction: The Spectacular Crash of the Record Industry in the Digital Age. By Steve Knopper (Free Press, 2009). This book traces the rise of the digital age in music and how the recording industry's refusal to embrace it led to its major crash.

Hit Men: Power Brokers and Fast Money Inside the Music Business. By Frederic Dannon (First Vintage Books, 1991). Published in the early 1990s, this is a bit of a classic about sleazy record promotion practices of the 1980s, including payola and other illegal methods the record industry used to get music played on the radio.

Off the Record: The Technology and Culture of Sound Recording in America. By David L. Morton (Rutgers University Press, 2000). Morton reviews the development of audio recording technologies, from wire spools to eight-track and DAT tapes. Each of his case studies dispels the popular notion that recording is all about music, and they tell a much more complete story of sound recording technology and history.

Perfecting Sound Forever: An Aural History of Recorded Music. By Greg Milner (Faber and Faber, 2009). Milner surveys developments in recording, from Thomas Edison's complaints about Victrolas to the contemporary controversy between CD and vinyl. He looks at the technicians and engineers behind the recorded sound and details the science behind wax, vinyl, magnetic tape, compact discs, and more.

Playback: From the Victrola to the MP3: 100 Years of Music, Machines, and Money. By Mark Coleman (Da Capo Press, 2003). This book provides a historical overview of the connection between music, technology, and the "systematic marketing of recorded music."

Ripped: How the Wired Generation Revolutionized Music. By Greg Kot (Scribner, 2009). A recap of the last 10 years concerning how digital technology transformed the music industry. The book covers the rise of Napster, the music industry's fight against file sharing, and how new artists are using the technology to reach more fans.

Selling Sounds: The Commercial Revolution in American Music. By David Suisman (Harvard University Press, 2009). From Tin Pan Alley to grand opera, player-pianos to phonograph records, this book explores the rise of music as big business and the creation of a new musical culture.

Books: Biographies
Folkways Records: Moses Asch and His Encyclopedia of Sound. By Tony Olmsted (Routledge, 2003). In 1949, immigrant recording engineer Moses Asch embarked on a lifelong project: documenting the world of sound produced by mankind, via a small record label called Folkways Records. By 1986, when Asch died, he had amassed an archive of over 2,200 LPs and thousands of hours of tapes; so valuable was this collection that it was purchased by the Smithsonian Institute. This is an account of how he built this business, against all odds—and against all conventional thinking and common sense.
Good Rockin' Tonight: Sun Records and the Birth of Rock 'n' Roll. By Colin Escott (St. Martin's Griffin, 1992). The Sun record label was founded by Sam Phillips in 1952. It was the first to record artists who blended country music with rhythm and blues (R & B), creating a "rockabilly" sound that set the direction for rock 'n' roll. This book recounts the tale of the label that discovered Elvis Presley, Jerry Lee Lewis, Johnny Cash, and Roy Orbison.
Here, There and Everywhere: My Life Recording the Music of the Beatles. By Geoff Emerick (Gotham, 2006). Emerick's career as a recording engineer began at age 15 when he worked with the Beatles as an assistant engineer at Abbey Road Studios. By 19, he became a full engineer, working the board for *Revolver* and *Sgt. Pepper's Lonely Hearts Club Band*. He came up with innovative recording techniques along the way, including using a loudspeaker as a microphone. This is his story of working with The Beatles.
Hitman: Forty Years of Making Music, Topping Charts, and Winning Grammys. By David Foster (Pocket, 2008). Foster recounts his career as a composer, songwriter, arranger, and record producer, working with artists such as Barbra Streisand, George Harrison, Paul McCartney, Diana Ross, Rod Stewart, Madonna, Toni Braxton, and Michael Jackson.
Inside the Recording Studio: Working with Callas, Rostopovich, Domingo, and the Classical Elite. By Peter Andry (Rowman &

Littlefield, 2008). Record producer Peter Andry recounts his experiences from over 50 years in the classical music industry, offering portraits of great singers, instrumentalists, and conductors such as Maria Callas, Yehudi Menuhin, and Herbert von Karajan.

Lost Sounds: Blacks and the Birth of the Recording Industry. By Tim Brooks and Dick Spottswood (University of Illinois Press, 2004). An in-depth history of the involvement of African Americans in the early recording industry that examines the first three decades of sound recording in the United States, charting the varied roles black artists played in the period.

Q: The Autobiography of Quincy Jones. By Quincy Jones (Harlem Moon, 2002). "I've been driven all my life by a spirit of adventure and a criminal level of optimism." Those words from Quincy Jones in his autobiography give you some idea of the driving personality of this prolific producer-arranger who produced Michael Jackson's smash album *Thriller*.

The Record Men: The Chess Brothers and the Birth of Rock & Roll. By Rich Cohen (Norton, 2005). The story of Leonard Chess and his recordings of Muddy Waters, Bo Diddley, and Chuck Berry.

Books: Technical Reference

101 Recording Tips: Stuff All the Pros Know and Use. By Adam St. James (Hal Leonard, 2004). St. James shares his tricks of the trade, garnered through a lifetime of home and pro studio recording. He passes on lessons learned firsthand from legendary producers, engineers, and artists such as Tom Dowd, Phil Ramone, Pete Anderson, Dick Shurman, Jeff Beck, Steve Vai, Joe Satriani, and Desmond Child.

The Art of Music Production. By Richard Burgess (Music Sales Corporation, 2005). Successful music producers share revealing anecdotes about the business and the stars, including how to deal with the big-ego artists, taking care of the legal aspects, and taping a great session.

The Art of Producing. By David Gibson (Artistpro, 2004). Gibson lays out a specific process for producing a music project from start to finish, including virtual recording, virtual instruments, vocal techniques, and MIDI tracking.

Handbook of Recording Engineering. By John Eargle (Springer, 2005). A hands-on book for aspiring recording engineers. Digital recording and signal processing are covered in detail.

Problem
Solving

Problem: A band comes in to record a session, but the bass player is mad at the drummer and storms out in the middle of the session. He sits in the hallway sulking for two hours, and all recording stops. As the session goes on, the band asks if you, the engineer, can play keyboard on a tune. You come up with a part and play a mini-organ on the song. When the session is over, you have put in way more hours and talent than expected, but the band just wants to pay you the price agreed upon. That original price was for fewer hours of work. How do you handle this?

Answer: Al Houghton, audio engineer and owner of Dubway Studios, says that you need to be clear with the artists who come in. "In this case, they're already paying for your engineering expertise, but now they take advantage of your musicianship and songwriting as well," says Houghton. "If you give this added service, you might say upfront that they are going to be charged. Some artists just expect you to work additionally for free, but you may say upfront that they should pay for your extra work." Also, Houghton points out that sometimes engineers and assistant engineers have to play the role of psychologist. Instead of wasting the studio time, he or an assistant engineer would have tried to talk to the bass player to smooth over the situation and get the players back performing.

Mixing Audio. By Roey Izhaki (Focal Press, 2008). An in-depth look at practices, concepts, tools, and instruments used in audio mixing.

Modern Recording Technique, 7th Edition. By David Miles Huber (Focal Press, 2009). A cover-to-cover reference manual for any recording professional. It covers everything from room acoustics to running a session.

Periodicals

American Songwriter Devoted to the art of songwriting, this magazine also has sections on technology and the music business. (http://www.americansongwriter.com)

Audio Media A magazine for audio production professionals that covers pro audio technology, technique, and business for the post, broadcast, recording, media authoring, sound reinforcement, location, and mastering markets. (http://www.audiomedia.com)

Billboard *Billboard* started as a publication that followed the popular music charts, printing the top-selling albums for the week. Since its inception in 1894, the magazine has evolved into a primary source of information on trends and innovation in music, serving music fans, artists, top executives, tour promoters, publishers, radio programmers, lawyers, retailers, digital entrepreneurs, and many others. (http://www.billboard.com)

EQ This source explains all new audio and home recording studio equipment and software. (http://www.eqmag.com)

Mix *Mix* is one of the leading magazines for the professional recording and sound production technology industry. *Mix* covers a wide range of topics including: recording, live sound and production,

Everyone Knows

According to the Freelancers Union, freelancers make up 30 percent of all workers, and in a down economy that number can go even higher. Many people working in the recording industry have to work on a freelance basis. Many recording engineers only find work on a project-to-project basis. Because many opportunities in this industry are for freelancers, many professionals have to:

- Network often to find work leads.

- Carefully track finances and make regular payments toward their income tax. Freelancers are running their own business, so they must keep track of all business expenses and receipts.

- Build an emergency fund. Work can ebb and flow, so freelancers need to build a reserve.

- Establish a fair but competitive work rate. You do not want to charge too little for your services and you do not want to price yourself out of work. Survey what other people charge and come up with a reasonable rate.

broadcast production, audio for film and video, and music technology. (http://www.mixonline.com)

MusicTech Magazine A British magazine for producers, engineers, and recording musicians, spotlighting recording tips and gear. (http://www.musictechmag.com.uk)

ProSound News Tons of industry news items on who's working where, new equipment, and trade shows. The industry calendar here helps to track major events in the business.   (http://www.prosoundnews.com)

Recording This magazine for the recording musician highlights reviews of new equipment, interviews with the engineers and producers who influence the way music is made today, and explanations of any new technology as it is introduced on the market. (http://www.recordingmag.com)

SoundonSound The music recording technology magazine delivers a mix of detailed, hands-on product tests of cutting-edge music hardware/software, covering all aspects of sound acquisition, editing, and playback. The publication also presents producer/ engineer/musician interviews and "how to" workshops and tutorials.   (http://www.soundonsound.com)

Other Media

Movies

Almost Famous (2000). Based on director Cameron Crowe's real life as a young writer for *Rolling Stone*, this film is a fun story about touring with a rock band.

Dreamgirls (2006). A fictionalized account of the rise of The Supremes and Motown, Jamie Foxx's character is Motown founder Berry Gordy and Beyoncé plays the Diana Ross role.

Grace of My Heart (1996). Set in the 1960s, the film is loosely based on the life of song writer Carole King and gives an account of what it was like to work in the Brill Building, where scores of music publishers had offices.

High Fidelity (2000). This comedy is for the record store owners and those who compulsively make lists about music and bands.

I'm Trying to Break Your Heart (2002). A documentary about the recording of Wilco's album *Yankee Hotel Foxtrot* shows a band in turmoil and gives a view into the band's conflict with its record label.

Ray (2004). The movie biography of Ray Charles with Jamie Foxx in the title role traces the music star's rise to fame.

This Is Spinal Tap (1984). This parody of a documentary about a heavy metal band is strictly for laughs, but malfunctioning props and a rapid descent from fame can be a real part of the music biz.

The Wrecking Crew (2008). A documentary about a group of 1960s studio musicians in Los Angeles who played for the Beach Boys, Frank Sinatra, Nancy Sinatra, Sonny and Cher, Jan & Dean, The Monkees, Gary Lewis and the Playboys, Mamas and Papas, Tijuana Brass, Ricky Nelson, Johnny Rivers, and helped Phil Spector create his "Wall of Sound."

Education

Berklee College of Music Concentrates on the study and practice of contemporary music, featuring more than a dozen majors in the practice and business of music. 1140 Boylston Street, Boston, Massachusetts, 02215, (800) 237-5533, (http://www.berklee.edu)

Full Sail University Features bachelor's degree programs in recording arts and in music business, as well as a master's program specializing in the entertainment industry. 3300 University Boulevard, Winter Park, Florida, 32792, (800) 226-7625, (http://www.fullsail.edu)

Institute of Audio Research Offers a 900-hour course that prepares students for entry-level careers in film, broadcast, and audio production. 64 University Place, New York, New York, 10003-4595, (800) 544-2501, (http://www.audioschool.com)

Institute of Production and Recording Founded in 2002 by a group of education and media professionals, the institute offers associate's degrees on both the production side and the business side of the recording industry. 312 Washington Avenue North, Minneapolis, Minnesota, 55401 (866) 477-4840, (http://www.ipr.edu)

Media Tech Institute The program in recording arts is designed to prepare students for entry-level work as engineers. 400 E. Royal Lane, Suite 100, Irving, TX 75039, (866) 498-1122, (http://www.mediatechinstitute.com)

Recording Engineers Institute Founded in 1973, this institution focuses on hands-on instruction of engineering techniques. 100-5 Patco Court, Islandia, New York, 11749, (631) 582-8999, (http://www.audiotraining.com)

UCLA Extension/Entertainment Studies & Performing Arts Department This comprehensive program offers more than 200 practical courses and certification opportunities and features well-developed interning and networking prospects. 10995 Le Conte Avenue, Room 437, Los Angeles, CA 90024-1333, (800) 825-9064, (http://www.uclaextension.edu/fos/entertainment.aspx)

Women's Audio Mission This nonprofit organization seeks to provide advanced training to women in the recording arts. 1890 Bryant Street, Suite 312, San Francisco, California, 94110, (415) 558-9200, (http://www.womensaudiomission.org)

Web Sites

General Industry Sites

Artistshouse Music This nonprofit, online organization gives informational support, guidance, and expert resources to help navigate challenges and maximize opportunities in the music industry. (http://www.artistshousemusic.org)

Just Plain Folks This site boasts membership of more than 51,500 songwriters, recording artists, and music industry professionals. The group offers a mentoring program and an extensive list of industry resources. (http://www.jpfolks.com)

KnowTheMusicBiz.com KnowTheMusicBiz.com is an online community and resource center for independent artists and musicians. The goal of this site is to help make available the

Fast Facts

A new career related to the recording industry is forensic audio specialist, a professional who provides objective, scientific examinaitons of recordings. The Institute for Forensic Audio in Colonia, New Jersey (http://www. owlinvestigations.com) offers certificates in video and audio authenticity and voice identification. The lab features an Avid Forensic workstation, which enables hands-on experience. Evidence procedures, legal questions, and courtroom testimony related to the above specialties are discussed.

information needed to build a sustainable career in the rapidly changing music industry.   (http://www.knowthemusicbiz.com)

Mix Makers: All Music Industry Contacts This site presents hundreds of music industry contacts; including record label A&R, music managers, agents, producers, and publishers. It is designed for independent record labels, singers, musicians, rappers, producers, managers, publishers, sound engineers, agents, major record labels, and distributors.   (http://allmusicindustrycontacts.com)

MusicBizAcademy.com This site is loaded with helpful articles on the business of selling, promoting, and making music on the Internet and other related music biz information.   (http://www.musicbizacademy.com)

Music Business Page This site claims to be the oldest online site about the music business, and it provides information about music business schools, pro sound effects libraries, music jobs, record production, and more.   (http://www.musicbusinesspage.com)

Music Dish MusicDish e-Journal features a business perspective on key issues sure to impact artists, labels, and fans. The site features a "Career Tips" section.   (http://www.musicdish.com)

MusiciansNews.com While this site is dedicated to instruments, artists and competitions, it features loads of details on musical gear and recording equipment.   (http://www.musiciansnews.com)

Music Tank A British network established to engage with industry, innovation, and change across the music business.   (http://www.musictank.co.uk)

RecordProduction.com A network for record producers, recording studios, recording engineers, students, and musicians. The site offers virtual recording studio tours and interviews with 192 music producers talking about how they do their job. Also, you will find career tips and advice on education.   (http://www.recordproduction.com)

Job Boards

AllAccess Music Group Register to find postings in the radio and recording industry.   (http://www.allaccess.com)

Backstagejobs.com This is an online source for behind the scenes jobs in entertainment.   (http://www.backstagejobs.com/jobs.htm)

CreativeJobsCentral.com This job site is dedicated to those seeking creative job positions.   (http://www.creativejobscentral.com)

EntertainmentCareers.net This Web site features entertainment jobs and internships listings at studios, networks, production companies, record companies, TV and radio stations, animation studios, and more.   (http://www.entertainmentcareers.net)

Los Angeles Music Network The network promotes career advancement and education among music industry professionals. (http://www.lamn.com)

MediaBistro This site highlights listings for media professionals. (http://www.mediabistro.com)

Music-Careers.com Job seekers connect with employers in the music industry on this site.   (http://www.music-careers.com)

MusiciansContact.com This online source connects musicians to paying jobs.   (http://www.musicianscontact.com)

Radio Online Find free listings for those seeking radio positions. (http://menu.radio-online.com/cgi-bin/rolmenu.exe/menu)

ShowbizJobs.com This site serves as a career center for entertainment professionals.   (https://www.showbizjobs.com)

Index

WITHDRAWN